hiking adventures with children

Southern Vancouver Island and the Olympic Peninsula

hiking
adventures
with children

KARI JONES AND SACHIKO KIYOOKA

Heritage
House

Cover and interior photos by Kari Jones and Sachiko Kiyooka.
Cover and interior design and layout by Sachiko Kiyooka.
Illustrations and maps by Joseph Hoh.
This book is set in Adobe Garamond, Humanist 777, and
Tahoma.

Library and Archives Canada Cataloguing in Publication

Jones, Kari, 1966-
    Hiking adventures with children: southern Vancouver
Island and the Olympic Peninsula / Kari Jones and Sachiko
Kiyooka.

ISBN 1-894384-86-5

    1. Hiking—British Columbia—Vancouver Island—
Guidebooks. 2. Hiking—Washington (State)—Olympic
Peninsula—Guidebooks. 3. Outdoor recreation for children—
British Columbia—Vancouver Island—Guidebooks. 4. Outdoor
recreation for children—Washington (State)—Olympic
Peninsula—Guidebooks. 5. Vancouver Island (B.C.)—
Guidebooks. 6. Olympic Peninsula (Wash.)—Guidebooks.
I. Kiyooka, Sachiko. II. Title.

GV199.44.C22V35 2005a   796.51'083'097112   C2005-900488-6

Heritage House acknowledges the financial support for its
publishing program from the Government of Canada through
the Book Publishing Industry Development Program (BPIDP),
The Canada Council for the Arts, and the Province of British
Columbia through the British Columbia Arts Council.

Heritage House Publishing Co. Ltd.
108 -17665 66A Avenue
Surrey, BC, Canada
V3S 2A7
greatbooks@heritagehouse.ca
www.heritagehouse.ca

Printed and bound in Canada

BRITISH COLUMBIA
ARTS COUNCIL
Supported by the Province of British Columbia

CONTENTS

1 Introduction 1
2 Knowing Your Family's Needs 5
3 All About Gear 11
4 What to Wear 21
5 Eating Well 29
6 Packing 37
7 No-Trace Trail Ethics 41
8 Home Away From Home 47
9 Safety Guidelines 53
10 On the Road 63

Introduction to Destinations 69

Day Trips

1 Coast Trail, East Sooke Regional Park 71
2 Centennial/High Ridge Loop, Francis/King Regional Park 76
3 Mt. Newton Loop, John Dean Provincial Park 80
4 Prospectors' Trail, Goldstream Provincial Park 86
5 Sandcut Beach, Western Forest Products Recreation Area 91
6 Witty's Beach Trail, Witty's Lagoon Regional Park 96

Overnights

7 Mystic Beach, Juan de Fuca Provincial Park 102
8 Ruckle Provincial Park, Saltspring Island 107
9 Sidney Spit Marine Park, Gulf Islands National Marine Park Reserve 116
10 Sombrio Beach, Juan de Fuca Provincial Park 125

Long Weekends

11 Carmanah Valley, Carmanah Walbran Provincial Park 134
12 Lake Helen Mackenzie, Strathcona Provincial Park 141
Olympic National Park (U.S.) Destinations 150
13 Upper Lake Mills, Olympic National Park 152
14 Rialto Beach to Ellen Creek, Olympic National Park 160

Checklists 170
First-Aid Guidelines 182
Recipes 186
Play and Learning Activities 191
Identification Guide 198
Maps, Books, and Websites 212

Destinations Location Map

1 **Coast Trail**
East Sooke Regional Park

2 **Centennial Loop**
Frances/King Regional Park

3 **Mt. Newton Loop**
John Dean Provincial Park

4 **Prospectors' Trail**
Goldstream Provincial Park

5 **Sandcut Beach**
Forest Recreation Area

6 **Witty's Beach Trail**
Witty's Lagoon Regional Park

7 **Mystic Beach**
Juan de Fuca Provincial Park

8 **Ruckle Park**
Ruckle Provincial Park

9 **Sidney Spit**
Gulf Islands National Marine Park

10 **Sombrio Beach**
Juan de Fuca Provincial Park

11 **Carmanah Valley**
Carmanah/Walbran Provincial Park

12 **Lake Helen Mackenzie**
Strathcona Provincial Park

13 **Upper Lake Mills**
Olympic National Park (Washington)

14 **Rialto Beach**
Olympic National Park (Washington)

Vancouver Island

12 Comox
Courtenay

Parksville

Tofino

Port Alberni

Lake Cowichan

11 Duncan

0   50 km

Port Renfrew

VANCOUVER ISLAND

Neah Bay

Victoria

Port Angeles

US HWY 101

Forks

13

14

WASHINGTON STATE

Olympic National Park

0   40 km

10

7

5

Jordan River

HWY 14

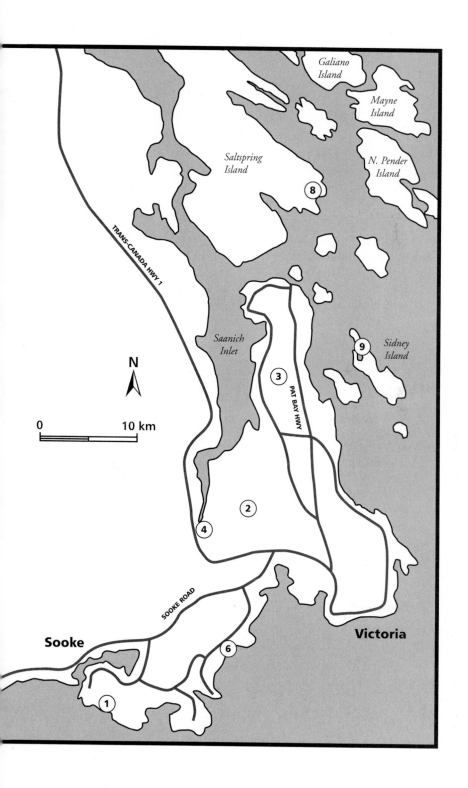

Galiano
Island

Mayne
Island

N. Pender
Island

Saltspring
Island

8

TRANS-CANADA HWY 1

Saanich
Inlet

9   Sidney
Island

3

PAT BAY HWY

N

0   10 km

2

4

SOOKE ROAD

Sooke

6

Victoria

1

ACKNOWLEDGEMENTS

We'd like to thank everyone who helped us with this book, encouraging us and offering guidance, information, and support, including: Frances Backhouse, who gave us feedback on our proposal and shared her publishing experience; Graham Shulley, who reviewed our natural history information; Grant Keddie of the Royal B.C. Museum, who graciously verified First Nations information and history; Rob Campbell and Sarah Williams for providing great details on the trails at Carmanah; Michael Pardy, for setting us right on safety issues; Joseph Hoh, for creating all the maps and beautiful illustrations; Dawn Jones, for her dedicated reading; Frances Hunter, for generously sharing her knowledge about book design and layout; and Karla Decker and Vivian Sinclair of Heritage House Publishing, for their friendly editorial support.

Most of all, thank you Rowan, Elena, and Marin for taking us by the hand, and letting us see the world through your eyes.

"If a child is to keep alive his inborn sense of
wonder ... he needs the companionship of
at least one adult who can share it, rediscovering
with him the joy, excitement and mystery
of the world we live in."

—Rachel Carson, *The Sense of Wonder*

1

INTRODUCTION

The earth keeps some vibration going
there in your heart, and that is you.

—Edgar Lee Masters

Being out of doors is not optional for us. It is how we replenish our souls. It is how we learn about the way the world works. Going hiking and camping is a way to get exercise, to gain a new perspective, to watch the seasons change. We fill ourselves with fresh air, sky, and the absence of a built environment. Our bodies relax, our minds empty, and our spirits open. We see places that are not visible from cars or buses, and have experiences that can only happen when we leave the television and radio behind. In the wilderness we talk more about things that are important to us; we spend more time in quiet contemplation. We spend uninterrupted time together and we often feel closer when we return.

We have walked, hiked, and gone wilderness camping in many places in the world, so when our children were born, we imagined we'd keep doing what we loved. Kari thought she would kayak in Clayoquot Sound with Rowan lying in the bottom of the kayak. Sachiko dreamed romantic thoughts of gypsy-like travel with babies wrapped onto her back. But the reality of life with infants and young children required some adjustments.

With small children to bring along, our challenge has been to stay focussed on the essence of what matters to us about being in the wild, and at the same time shift our expectations to account for the new needs of a young family.

If the most important thing about being "away" is being together and being "in nature," then we consider where a two-year-old can play safely and where an adult might find a contemplative walk. Babies, toddlers, and six-year-olds have different transportation, supervision, and play needs. Being realistic about the desires and limitations of each family member allows us to plan trips that make the presence of young children a gift, not a burden.

When Rowan says, "Mummy, the trees are singing," or Elena proudly shows us her anemone drawings, witnessing our children access the peace and wonder we have found in nature reminds us that that we don't have to travel to the highest mountaintop or venture to a far-flung corner of the world to see and to share the gifts of the natural world with each other. Our children's delight in the tiniest treasure helps us to open our eyes again wide, to see all that is right here before us.

About the book

When we first began working together, we sat down one afternoon on a straw mat in Sachiko's living room and talked about some of our dreams. As fate would have it, we both envisioned writing a hiking/camping book for families with young children! Surprised and delighted to find ourselves kindred spirits, we realized we could collaborate, and *Hiking Adventures with Children* was born.

Ruckle Park, Saltspring Island

We envisioned a resource that was written with parents and young children in mind—frank, practical, and filled with actual first-hand parent experiences, where one could quickly find hikes suited to the specific needs of parents with preschoolers, with all the information on hand to make planning quick, easy, and even fun. We thought our ultimate hiking book for young families would make good bedside reading as well, with funny and inspiring anecdotes to skim through on a wet January evening.

The content of *Hiking Adventures with Children* reflects the many facets of information that we wish to share with our children. As parents, we become our children's guides, interpreters, and safety monitors. We set the tone for outings and help shape the way our children learn about the natural world. For us, and for many other parents we know, it is important to speak knowledgeably about the natural and human history of the areas we are in. Our children learn to share our inquisitiveness and appreciation of the land that is our home.

We have included First Nations history for each of our destinations, something we have found missing in other guidebooks, and which we feel is very important. The forests and beaches we explore were home to diverse First Nations peoples for thousands of years before European settlement, and we want to share with our children the knowledge that Aboriginal peoples lived in harmony with the natural world for many, many generations before us.

We hope *Hiking Adventures with Children* makes it easy for you to plan and enjoy getting away to the wild with your young children. The first chapter, "Knowing Your Family's Needs," will help you reflect on how to make your outdoor adventures satisfying for everyone. If you have already done a lot of wilderness hiking, gear, trail ethics, and good practises may already be second-nature. If you are new to this, then our chapters covering everything from gear to no-trace trail ethics and safety will provide lots of information and tips to get you started. You'll also find help in planning what to eat and how to pack everything, and at the end of the book are convenient checklists for getting and staying organized.

About the destinations

This book is *not* for hard-core hiker-parents. Because of their very high level of commitment, preparation, and experience, these folks, once parents, will find ways to continue doing long or difficult trips, babe (or toddler) on their back or at their side. We have read the amazing account of a couple who logged 2,100 miles hiking *with* their infant daughter (see *Kids in the Wild* by Cindy Ross and Todd Gladfelter). Our aims are more modest.

We *are* interested in the most low-impact, no-trace experience we can have close to home with babies and preschool-age children. We don't like to share the night sky with Top 40 radio or be surrounded by creature comforts. We have chosen our special places because they are easily accessible on child-friendly trails and offer walk-in camping in beautiful locations that are generally quiet and not overcrowded.

Even though these destinations may not provide the same physical challenges or take us as far into the wilderness as we might go on an adult hike, they give us the opportunity to introduce our children first-hand to the gifts of the natural world. We know that this stage of parenthood will not last forever and that as our children grow older, we will be able to wander farther afield with them.

The destinations we have included are our personal favourites for day, overnight, and long-weekend getaways. The day hikes are just a few of many possibilities in the region (these are well documented in a number of other walking/trail guides), but they are the ones we love to go back to because they are fun for our children and pleasing to us. The overnights are easily accessible destinations where families can tent on a peaceful beach, bluff, or meadow and never hear a car. The long weekends are more challenging trips that involve a longer journey and more planning, but will take you to beautiful, less-travelled alpine and subalpine meadows, ancient rainforests, or unspoiled coastlines on Vancouver Island and in Washington's Olympic National Park, just a short ferry ride south of Victoria.

The trips extend north, south, east, and west of Victoria in no more than a four-hour driving radius, with the day trips and overnights averaging no more than an hour and a half of driving time. Only the long-weekend destinations involve more than two hours in the car. Of course, you can also make our overnight destinations into long weekends.

Happy trails!

We hope that *Hiking Adventures with Children* will be indispensable to you at home, en route, and on the trail. When you reach your special place, you can use the identification guide in the back of the book to identify trees, flowers, animals, birds, and intertidal life. You can use or adapt activities we've listed for keeping little ones happy and motivated whether you are walking in to your camping meadow, exploring the new environment, or in the tent getting ready to go to sleep.

We are looking forward to using *Hiking Adventures with Children* more than anyone else! Now we won't have to find that crumpled piece of loose-leaf on which we scribbled our last packing list. We won't be growing frustrated on the trail trying to conjure ideas for encouraging Rowan, Elena, and Marin onward to trail's end. And we won't be looking at the fantastic little creatures on the beach, unable to identify them. We'll have our very own companion copies of *Hiking Adventures with Children* in our jacket pockets.

We wish you happy adventures in the wild with your babies, toddlers, and preschoolers. See you on the beach, in the mountains, and along the forest paths.

2 KNOWING YOUR FAMILY'S NEEDS

The problem is not that there are problems.
The problem is expecting otherwise and
thinking that having problems is a problem.

—Theodore Rubin

Why are you doing this?

We all have different reasons for being in nature. Some people like to get out to feel the quiet and calm. Some choose hiking and camping as a way to challenge themselves physically. Some like the way being on a beach or hiking a path slows them down and makes them take a look around. In fact, there are as many reasons for getting out in nature as there are people.

If you hiked BC (before children), you may need to rethink the "why" of hiking *with children*. You can still seek quiet and natural beauty, but you likely won't be hiking steep mountainsides or putting in full days with lots of mileage.

We value and love the natural world, and we hope that by sharing positive experiences with our children, they too will grow to love the wild as much as we do. We also want to get away from our routines and our too-familiar environments. And maybe most importantly, being out in the wild is a way to spend time together, to know one another in new ways, and to share experiences that become family memories.

Outdoor play has many benefits

Curiosity. The wild is a wonderful backdrop for our children's natural curiosity, stimulating them in new and wonderful ways. "Why?" is aroused by the incredible diversity of creatures, plants, earth, and sky on one hand, and the complex set of relationships that support that diversity.

Physical coordination. The outdoors encourages our children's physical development. Playgrounds are simple representations of the tangle of logs, roots, branches, and streams of the natural world.

Action–Consequence. There is a clear line between action and consequence in the wild, which makes it easier for children to connect the two. In other settings, these lines are less evident. Because of the clear

A helping hand at Francis/King Park

link in the natural world, it is much easier to talk in concrete terms about respect for nature, respect for others, and self-respect.

Education. There are many lessons to be learned in the wild—natural science, social relations, problem solving, aesthetic appreciation, ethics, motivation, spirituality, and much more.

Realistic expectations

When it comes to creating a positive experience for all family members, expectations are everything—realistic expectations. Choices about where to go, how far to hike, how long to stay, what to bring—all depend on the children, their age, and their temperament.

Babies must be carried. Toddlers are discovering the power of their free will and may choose to teeter along slowly, try to keep up with older siblings, or flat-out refuse to walk a single step. They need constant supervision. Generally, older children (three and up) are more physically capable of negotiating varied terrain but may not all have the desire to hike long distances.

Some children are just naturally more physical than others and might enjoy a demanding hike through mud and over tree roots, while others would take one look and say, "I want to go home." Choose your destination carefully, knowing the kind of people your children are.

Zen and the art of slowing down

Sachiko's family once day-hiked with a friend and her two-year-old son. Sean wanted to walk by himself. Every couple of steps down the trail, he found something fascinating that required close and lengthy examination. All the adults were consequently walking at a snail's pace, too.

A slower pace can be very frustrating if you expect to go faster and are focussed on the "destination." The key is—don't expect to go faster. As the Taoist saying goes: "The journey is the reward." This is an opportunity to see the gift in the smallest of things and to marvel along with a child who is discovering the natural world for the first time. Throw out the idea that *distance* is one of the main goals in a hike and replace it with a simpler goal: simply being in nature with your children and giving them the opportunity to discover it for themselves.

Motivation and encouragement

You know how far it is to the destination and how long it will take to get there. But for children who live in the present, all they know is that they are here now, and they are not there yet! If your children get discouraged, or are tired, cold, wet, hungry, bored, or scared, be assured that no one will be happy! Follow these guidelines for a successful trip:
* Let older children help choose the destination.
* Try to choose a destination with an exciting point of interest like a beach, a waterfall, a look-out point, etc.
* Team up with another family or bring along a friend for your child—having a companion can make a lot of difference.
* Start early in the day when everyone is fresh.
* Keep everyone warm and dry.
* Let children lead the group (be sure to teach them trail safety as part of this).
* Take frequent breaks.
* Carry more water than you think you'll need.
* Bring plenty of snacks.
* Pack and save a few special "rewards" for when you really need them!
* Play games to keep interest up (see the back of this book for ideas).
* Give lots of praise and encouragement.

Always have a Plan B. If you are day-hiking, you can turn around and head back at any time. There is no dishonour in this! Better to have a short, enjoyable outing than to push children and make them

Hiking profiles

Baby (0 – 18 months)
Maximum distance: You'll be carrying *them*—how far can *you* walk supporting 10 – 25 pounds and anything else you need to carry?
Terrain: Whatever you can handle (know your own limitations).
An undemanding hiker! Easy-care for the most part. Just needs a willing adult to carry her, as well as proper clothing and protection from the weather so she's comfortable. Can go any distance as long as the parent is up to it.

Toddler (18 – 36 months)
Maximum distance: Unassisted, maybe 1 or 2 km, very slowly; carried, depends on the parent (again, know your own limitations).
Terrain: Easy to moderate trails only.
Expect to slow right down and live in the moment! A toddler will be the boss as far as pacing goes. Toddlers are happy to walk short distances, but their meandering pace can frustrate adults. If you are going more than a kilometre, expect to alternately carry them and have them walk on their own.

Preschooler (3 – 5 years)
Maximum distance: 7 km, depending on terrain and weather.
Terrain: Difficult trails may be possible, depending on your child.
Depending on your child's size, physical strength, and temperament once he reaches the preschool years, he will be ready for longer, more challenging hikes. How long? It depends on the child. We have found that 4 km is a good average distance for this age group.

regret the whole experience. You can be sure that will be counterproductive to your goal of wanting to instill a love of the wild in your children.

If you are backpacking or even just camping a short distance from the car, a bad-weather backup plan is a must-have. We've included backup suggestions for the overnight destinations in this book.

Taking time to meet everyone's needs

Try to plan a trip that will meet at least some of every family member's needs. Have a discussion about what everyone wants to do. If you talk about making compromises beforehand and build in time for each family member to do something they enjoy, you will avoid problems later.

During one discussion with our children about their camping trip goals, five-year-old Rowan said, "To be with you, play, and see whales." Six-year-old Elena's goals were "seeing different kinds of sceneries and wildlife, having time together, and having a fire." Two-year-old Marin's goals were "playing, running, chasing, and fishing."

If some members want to hike and others don't, you can split up for a while. The other family members can explore tide pools or look for wildlife, or sit in the tent and read books.

One of the most challenging things for parents on family outings is finding some time for themselves. With your partner or with some of the other adults, plan to take turns being away from the children so that each of you can have a few moments to explore your own interests. Going day-

Playing at the edge of Carmanah Creek

hiking or overnight camping with another family can make it easier for everyone to have time on their own. Children may play longer and more independently with playmates along, and parents can spell each other off—you might even get to go for a walk with just your partner!

Planning for everyone

- What does each family member enjoy most about being out in nature?
- What does each family member find the most challenging?
- How is everyone feeling? Are family members energetic, tired, adventuresome, fragile, or...?
- What are some of the features of destinations the family has enjoyed going to in the past?

Feeling safe

Kari's husband is a professional hiking and kayaking guide, and many years ago, when they first started exploring together, Michael always organized the trips. They met his needs well, but sometimes (okay—often) they took Kari out of her safe zone, past challenge … and into fear.

Rising to the challenge of an adventure is one thing when it is two consenting adults, but when children are involved, letting them be afraid is the best way to make them want to turn right around and head home.

Take your children's fears seriously and address them right away. Sometimes it simply requires explaining why or how something will happen. If the child's fear does not go away, try exploring it with them at their own pace, but always be prepared to turn around and leave behind whatever the child was fearful of, even if this means returning home. If this happens, try to get out again as soon as possible—probably to a different spot—and gently try again.

3

ALL ABOUT GEAR

"I think," said Christopher Robin,"that we
ought to eat all our provisions, so we won't
have so much to carry."

—A.A. Milne

Figuring out what to take on a trip can be overwhelming. Day hikes
are pretty simple, but what about overnights or longer trips? Do you
have everything you need? Having a family gear list keeps forgetting to
a minimum. Use the lists at the end of this book as your base, and add
your own items. Make your first overnight a test run at a nearby destination so that you can rush home if the tent leaks or if you didn't bring
enough diapers.

Child carrier

If your children are under three, you will likely be carrying them much
(if not all) of the time. For infants, a kangaroo-style front pack works
well. It should have a padded adult harness and hip belt to stabilize
your load and protect the lower back. For a baby who can sit without
support, or a toddler, use a backpack-style carrier. It's worth investing
in a good one. When we weren't hiking, we used ours all the time at
home for doing housework, or just out and about town.

Look for these features in a good child carrier:
- *Aluminum frame.*
- *Padded hip belt* (so you can shift the pack's weight
  for maximum ease and comfort).
- *Adjustable adult shoulder straps* so that anyone, whether
  big or small, can use it.
- *Lumbar pad*, adjustable to fit adults of varying torso
  lengths.
- *Padded sling seat* for baby with side leg openings.
- *Padded top* (where baby's head will rest).
- *Shoulder harness and seat belt.*

Kari and two-year-old Rowan on the trail

- *Hinged kickstand* with a wide tripod base.
- *Sun/rain canopy.* This is very helpful in wet weather and when it is hot and there is little shade.

Day pack

Hiking with young children means you are carrying all your stuff and theirs too. If one parent is carrying an infant or toddler, you will have a single day pack for the whole family—get one that is large enough to carry your first-aid kit, snacks, extra clothing, water, and emergency items. Look for the following:

- *Wide hip belt* (more than two inches) with some padding, to help you bear the weight of a full day pack.
- *External pockets* for easy access to maps, snacks, etc.
- *Internal pockets* for car keys, wallet, or other small items.
- *An exterior loop or mesh pocket* so you can store your water bottle upright and away from other items that need to stay dry.
- *Loops you can use to lash on extra items* as needed (like a wet rain jacket).
- *Adequate size* for carrying all your first-aid equipment, food, and extra clothes for all family members.

Backpack

If you are going away overnight or for a long weekend, remember that even if the car is only an hour away, carrying gear for any time in uncomfortable packs can be agony.

There are all kinds of manufacturers making backpacks. Before buying anything new, do your homework. Ask knowledgeable friends. Look on the internet. Check out several stores and have staff show you the pros and cons of different models. Once you've got a backpack and have adjusted it properly to fit your body, load up gear at home and do a test run to look for sore spots. Make sure you can comfortably carry the weight.

When choosing a backpack, look for:

- *A good hip belt* that fits and has enough stiffness to help you support the pack's load without sagging.
- *Well-constructed shoulder straps.* No puckering—these can turn into blisters when they sit against your skin on the trail.
- *Adjustable stabilizer straps* so you can adjust the pack to fit the length of your back.
- *A capacity that meets your needs.* How much will you need to carry? Will you be able to lift it when it is full? In both of our families, the men have larger packs because they are able to carry more.

- *An easy-access top pocket* or other exterior pocket. Many backpacks now have "lids" that zip off and become fanny packs or day packs. If you choose well, you may get two in one!

Tent

In some ways the tent is the most important piece of equipment for overnight camping— an essential part of your "camping house." It is where you sleep, where infants take naps or have quiet play, and it may need to house the whole family if the weather turns nasty.

There are many tents on the market, from cheap ones to high-end models. If you intend to make tenting part of your family lifestyle, avoid cheap tents that will not last more than a season, and that probably lack the features you need to keep everyone dry in our rainy climate.

Cozy in the tent at Sombrio Beach

When our families chose tents, we were concerned about balancing size and weight. We needed room for everyone, and we needed to be able to carry our tents on backpacking trips.

We both chose compact dome tents with full-length flies and vestibules that are roomy enough to store gear, but are not so big as to be very heavy. Kari's three-person family tent weighs 2.7 kg, while Sachiko's four-person tent weighs in at 4.5 kg (both at the heavier end for backpacking tents).

There are many things to look for when investing in a tent:
- *A double-wall design* (separate canopy and rain fly). Keeps rain out, breathes well and is warmer. Because the rain fly is separate, if it is damaged it can be repaired or replaced without having to buy a new tent. A full-length fly is essential for the best rain protection.

- *Fabric with UV protection.* Sun causes fabric to break down and eventually deteriorate, so UV protection is desirable. Keeping the rain fly on will provide added protection.
- *Attached floor with polyurethane coating.* Get quality! When the ground is wet, pressure from your body can force water through the tiniest weakness in floor fabric. A good floor keeps out moisture and is less susceptible to punctures.
- *A vestibule.* Protects the tent door from precipitation that can leak at zipper points and seams, provides a place to strip off wet clothing before getting in the tent, and gives you a dry area outside the tent to store footwear and other gear. Look for a vestibule supported with a pole because this gives better headroom.
- *Mesh windows that can be covered by nylon panels.* When open, these let out condensation in warm weather. When closed, they keep in the warmth.
- *Inside pockets* are very useful for keeping track of flashlights, matches, glasses, etc.
- *Adequate space.* Make sure you have enough room for everyone in your family. Test in the store by adding sleeping pads, bags, and family members! If you might want to bring a friend along on some of your trips, allow extra space.
- *Sealed seams and good seam design.* Fully taped seams are more waterproof than partially taped. Make sure you know which seams have been sealed by the manufacturer and ask about a seam-sealing kit so you can seal the rest yourself. If additional sealant is needed, ask how often it should be applied.
- *Easy set-up.* Can one person get the tent up with minimal assistance? With small children underfoot, you want a tent that can go up quickly and that doesn't require complex steps (that you might forget).
- *Reasonable weight.* If you will be doing any overnights that involve backpacking, weight is very important. Anything in excess of 5 kg is too heavy and bulky for backpacking.

Groundsheet

A groundsheet is a sheet of water-resistant material that goes underneath your tent. You can purchase one or make your own by buying plastic sheeting and cutting it to fit the footprint of your tent.

A groundsheet extends the life of the tent by reducing wear on the tent floor. First, it keeps the tent bottom clean. Secondly, it protects the tent floor from punctures (a new groundsheet is cheaper than a new tent). Finally, groundsheets are usually more waterproof than tent floors. Moisture from below accumulates on the groundsheet, rather than the tent, leaving your tent drier. When you are ready to pack up and move on, it is easier to deal with a wet groundsheet than to pack a wet tent.

Tarp

Because we live on the rainy west coast, the second essential part of the "camping house" is a tarp (or a couple of tarps). In addition to serving as backup if your tent leaks, a tarp provides you with a roomy, covered area, so you aren't confined to a tiny tent in the event of lots of rain. You can store gear, prepare and eat meals, play games, have some space to hang out—and still keep dry.

Tarps also come in many varieties. The cheapest (made from woven nylon) work as well as any other to keep out rain, but are very bulky. Specialized outdoor stores carry more expensive lightweight tarps suitable for hiking.

Like a good tent, a good-quality tarp is a worthwhile investment if you plan to do regular backpacking and camping. Choose a tarp according to your means, but remember you will need rope to secure it to trees. If you are not certain there will be trees, don't forget to bring a ski pole or a walking stick to use as a pole.

Catenary-shape tarp (above) and rectangle tarp (below)

Ask yourself these questions when considering a tarp:

- Is it the right size? Will it cover your tent as an emergency fly? Will it provide enough space if you need to set up a dry kitchen/eating/storage area?
- Is it easy to pack? Do you have room for it in your backpack if you are hiking a long distance?
- Can ropes be easily attached? Look for rivets where rope can be attached. If there are none, how will you secure ropes?

Sleeping bags

Unless the weather is very warm, it typically is too cold in this region to make do with cheap fleece- or wool-lined bags. Look for a good-quality bag that has either down or synthetic filling.

When Kari and her husband Michael go camping, they take one of each. Michael, who is a hot person, uses the synthetic, and Kari, who is always cold, uses the down. Because down loses its warmth when wet, Kari always packs her sleeping bag in a double layer of waterproof bags.

Children can use adult- or child-sized bags. The advantage of a child-sized bag is that it will be lighter to carry and will provide just the insulation a child needs with no excess. Don't skimp on a child's sleeping bag—novelty bags decorated with cartoon characters will *not* be adequate.

Look for these features in a sleeping bag:

- *Temperature rating.* Make sure you get a bag that will meet the weather conditions you expect—and then some. Three-season bags (-2 to -12°C) will carry you through spring, summer, and fall camping.
- *High loft.* "Loft" measures the "puffiness" of a sleeping bag—generally the loftier, the warmer.
- *Balance of warmth/weight/bulk to meet your needs.* Down bags are warmer, lighter, and compress well, but they are more expensive and less able to retain warmth if they get wet. Synthetic bags are less expensive, but bulkier and heavier. They are better insulators than down when wet.
- *Shape.* Mummy bags are warmer and more compact, but some people find them constricting.
- *Zip-together option.* Some bags can zip together, making one larger bag to share. This can be handy, especially if you are sleeping with an infant.

Sleeping pads

Blue foam sleeping pads are cheap, safe, and easy to use. Because they will not puncture, they can double as sitting mats outdoors, but they don't provide much insulation against the cold.

Self-inflating mats, such as Therm-A-Rests, are more expensive and provide better padding and better insulation. However, they can be easily punctured by sharp stones or sticks.

Camp stoves

For backpacking, the one-burner stove is the only way to go. We both have liquid-fuel stoves that burn white gas. The gas is stored in fuel bottles, which are refillable (best environmental option). These are the best bet if you will be doing frequent backcountry trips. You need to learn how to prime, light, pump, and clean the stove.

If you only plan to backpack occasionally, you can get a canister-style stove. They are super-convenient to use (just light and cook), but canisters are not refillable. If you will not

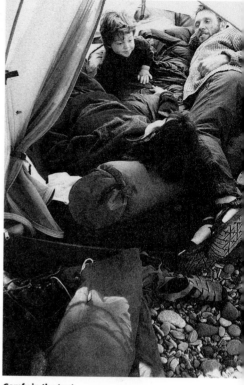

Comfy in the tent

be backpacking at all, you might want to use a heavier, two-burner stove.

Before buying or borrowing any stove, make sure you get a demo on how to operate it, and practise before you head off on a trip. It can be tricky to light fuel-bottle stoves, so be sure you know exactly what you are doing.

fuel-bottle stove

canister stove

two-burner stove

Kitchen gear

Cooking pots. You can invest in lightweight nesting pots especially designed for hiking or just pick up compact pots at a garage sale or thrift store. Small- to medium-size high-sided pots are best for one-pot cooking and do double duty for carrying water and as a sink. Don't use home cookware: it will become blackened from cooking over an open flame.

Frugal tip: if you get a thrift-store pot, choose one that allows you to unscrew the handle, which can be bulky and hard to pack. Then invest a few dollars in a portable pot gripper, available from outdoor stores.

Plates, cups, utensils. Keep it simple. We bring a bowl, an insulated cup, and a fork and spoon for each person. Plastic yogurt containers and plastic cutlery work well. A single pocket knife can do the trick for cutting and spreading foods.

Food prep and storage. For food prep, you can buy a small, lightweight cutting board made out of thin nylon or just make your own by cutting open a large plastic yogurt container to make a rectangle. Little plastic bottles with screw-on lids are handy for miscellaneous things like soya sauce, vinaigrette, cooking oil, spices, etc. No fancy gear is necessary for storing larger items—zip-lock bags and plastic food containers from home work very well.

Emergency gear

See Chapter 9 for details on emergency gear.

Flight test

Before an overnight trip, check your gear:

- Does the stove work?
- Is there enough fuel?
- Do flashlights work?
- Are there extra batteries?
- Are the knives sharp?
- Is the tent clean and rip-free?

- Do the tent seams need sealing?
- Are the sleeping bags clean and their loft fluffed?
- Are there any leaks in mattresses?
- Do packs have any tears, missing clasps or buckles, or cracks in the frame?
- Have the first-aid medications passed their expiry dates?
- Have you replaced any first-aid items that were used last time?

Caring for gear at home

Once you return home, clean and pack gear away properly so that it is ready to use the next time.

- Clean out and dry backpacks and tent.
- Unzip all compartments.
- Shake out and sponge interior with mild soap and water.
- Check for wear and tear.
- Replace any worn parts. Tears can be fixed with a heavy needle and upholstery thread. Fraying nylon can be mended by melting edges with a lighter or match.
- Store in a cool, dry place. Never store tents damp or wet; the fabric will be ruined.
- Shake out sleeping bags and store loosely in a large bag. If you store the sleeping bag in a stuff sack, the down fibres will be compressed and will eventually break apart.

Helping dad do repairs on a sunny afternoon at home

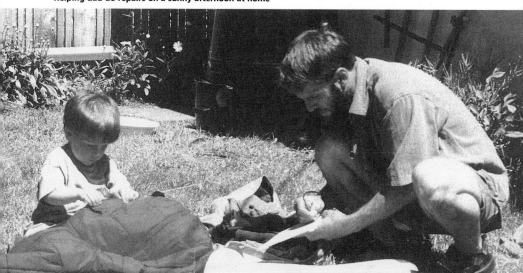

4

WHAT TO WEAR

*Know first who you are,
and then adorn yourself accordingly.*

— Euripides

We have learned over the years that having the right clothing can make a trip. Really! Being comfortable—especially warm and dry—is essential for everyone, parents and little ones alike.

Even if you are a natural-fibre type (like we are), synthetics are superior for hiking and wilderness camping. Why? Synthetic fabrics are lighter, provide excellent insulation, and dry *much faster* than natural fibres. Some examples of synthetics are polypropylene, Thermax, Capilene, and fleece, as well as polyester and nylon. Check labels. Virtually all outdoor clothing is now made with combinations of these types of fabrics.

Cotton has *no* insulating value and can take days to dry. We have hung wet cotton socks out for several overcast days and had to put them back on wet because they never did dry (a recipe for blisters). Don't bring cotton pants or jeans, socks, or sweatshirts. Not only will they be a nightmare to dry, they are heavy to carry. New, brushed synthetics feel and act like cotton, offering both breathability and quick-dry convenience. Look for them in specialty outdoor-clothing stores.

Wool socks and sweaters are definitely good insulators, but like cotton, they can be slow to dry if they get wet. Look for the new spun wools, which are much thinner and dry faster.

Layering

Layering is the secret to packing light and still ensuring you have clothes to handle all weather possibilities. By packing several lightweight layers, you can add and subtract layers as you need to.

In colder weather, we each usually hike wearing a long-sleeved synthetic shirt with a fleece jacket or wool sweater over top. For our legs we put on synthetic leggings or a pair of lightweight microfibre pants. We keep our waterproof jackets and pants handy in case it rains (or to

Hiking is fun even in winter with good raingear

use as an additional layer if we are cold).

In warmer weather, we often hike wearing a synthetic T-shirt and quick-dry synthetic shorts. As it gets cooler (when the sun goes down or if a cool wind picks up), we add a fleece long-sleeved top or wool sweater and a pair of microfibre pants or synthetic leggings.

For every trip, regardless of the current weather conditions and the forecast, we always pack *all* warm clothing and raingear. Evenings and early mornings are always cool, and in general, weather is very changeable; it is essential to be prepared. Even in summer, weather can turn chillingly cold.

Over 80 percent of heat loss occurs from the extremities—head, hands, and feet. Keep hat, gloves, and dry socks handy day and night for a quick warm-up.

Kari finds that Rowan is able to get wet in whatever she brings (he has a natural affinity for water—especially puddles!), so she always packs one extra coat for him and keeps it aside until absolutely necessary.

Best bets in clothing

For short day hikes in the summer, we don't always wear the ideal hiking clothing (we might just wear our regular shorts and T-shirts), but we always use the following guidelines when dressing for a cool-weather day hike or when packing for an overnight. See the back of the book for complete clothes-packing checklists.

TOPS

- Short-sleeved synthetic T-shirts or tank tops.
- Long-sleeved synthetic T-shirts.
- Fleece sweatshirts (with hoods, if possible) or wool sweaters.

BOTTOMS

- Synthetic or fleece leggings.
- Microfibre pants.
- Quick-dry synthetic shorts.

OUTERWEAR

- Rainpants.
- Raincoat.
- Lightweight windbreaker.

HEAD AND HANDS

- Fleece toque (not necessary if your fleece top has a hood) or balaclava (best hat for warm sleeping and can be used to wrap up a baby).
- Stretchy gloves (the little "magic" gloves are inexpensive and work well).
- Sun hat with a wide brim.

FEET

- Thin synthetic socks.
- Thicker wool- or nylon-blend socks.
- Comfortable, worn-in shoes, preferably with ankle support.

Frugal Finds

High-end specialty clothing is available if you can afford it, but with some advance planning, you don't need to spend a lot of money on clothing. We scout garage sales and thrift shops, where we have found, at great prices, like-new preschooler-sized fleece leggings from Mountain Equipment Co-op and kids' Gore-Tex jackets and good-quality rainpants. We buy synthetic tops and synthetic children's pants from thrift stores.

Layering basics

The three basic layers are:

- **Wicking layer.** To wick away moisture from the skin. This should be a long- or short-sleeved synthetic undershirt and synthetic leggings or light-weight microfibre pants. If you wear cotton next to your skin, the cotton will retain moisture, and you will get cold.
- **Insulating layer(s).** To keep you warm. A long-sleeved synthetic top or a fleece jacket.
- **Outer shell.** To protect from wind and rain. A waterproof jacket and pants or a rainsuit. (For young children, a one-piece rainsuit is great, but for older children, two pieces are easier to take off quickly—especially important during toilet training!)

They are not trendy-looking, but they do the job nicely. And we no longer scorn those ugly nylon socks we often receive at Christmas; they are great for hiking. You can also swap or buy second-hand from friends. Children outgrow clothing fast in the preschool years.

Pyjamas

For our younger children, we bring along fleece one-piece sleepers. These are perfect for multi-use: cozy at night, and in the morning, just add a jacket layer and children can get out of the tent in a jiffy for a quick trip to the bathroom. Our children have been known to wear them all day! Of course, in very warm weather, a T-shirt and under-wear are sometimes all anyone needs.

We all usually wear socks to bed. For children, this is important, especially if they are prone to throw off covers. If we get too hot and kick the socks off, they are easy to locate in the morning somewhere in the foot of the sleeping bag.

Keeping babies comfy

Babies are best dressed in layers like everyone else. If it is cold, make sure there is a windproof outer layer (one-piece rainsuits are excellent) and adequate insulating layers (again, one-piece outfits like fleecy blanket sleepers are great). If you are carrying a baby in a backpack, remember that while you might be warm because *you* are getting a workout, your baby might need an extra insulating layer because she isn't moving much or creating her own body heat.

It can be hard to find well-fitting mittens or gloves for small children and babies. If you don't have any, you can use synthetic socks. These

---

Best things to spend money on

- **Good-quality rainjacket and rainpants**. In the Pacific Northwest, raingear is a logical investment. For jackets, Gore-Tex–type fabrics are ideal. They are waterproof *and* breathable, and offer wind and rain protection as well as warmth. Rubberized jackets are adequate for shorter hikes, but because they don't "breathe," they trap moisture (sweat) inside and can contribute to making you feel cold.
- **A pair of synthetic leggings or microfibre pants**. These can be harder to find second-hand, but are necessities.
- For adults only—a pair of **good-quality, lightweight hiking boots.**

stretch well, so you can fit them over jacket cuffs. To be sure you don't lose them, sew them onto a piece of yarn and thread it through baby's jacket.

In hot weather, make sure babies are well protected from the sun with a wide-brimmed hat—and if you will be carrying your baby for some time in a child carrier, ensure baby's arms and legs are covered to prevent sunburn. Sun protection is just as important for older children; make sure

Playing at the water's edge at East Sooke Park

they keep hats on and are well protected with sunscreen or a long-sleeved shirt.

Tip: To keep a baby's hat on, use a string and tie it both to the hat and to your child carrier. If baby pulls the hat off (our children all *hated* wearing hats!), you won't have to backtrack down the trail to recover it. Use the same technique with toddlers who are prone to pull off their headgear. Fasten a string to the hat with a safety pin, and pin the string to the child's shirt. Be careful to use a string short enough that the child cannot wrap it around her neck.

What about diapers?
Just about all the hiking parents we know have a diaper disaster story. Friends have told Kari about running out of diapers and having to use an extra T-shirt someone had brought along. One friend sent her husband all the way back to the car and into town to buy some when they ran out. Then there was the time Kari's family got all the way to camp and realized they had forgotten to bring any diapers at all.

When planning a trip with a baby in diapers, remember:
- *Anything you pack in has to be packed out.* No diapers are disposable on the trail!
- *Don't take too many diapers.* Estimate how many you go through in a day, then add three to five more, per day. Don't forget to account for the time you won't be on the trail, but will be in transit. Clean diapers can be neatly stored in a nylon stuff sack.
- *Carry plastic bags for dirty diapers* (make sure they have no holes!) and an extra plastic bag to carry all the accumulated bags of dirty diapers.

- *If the weather is fine, practise prevention.* Consider letting your child be bare-bottomed on the beach or in camp.
- *Carry a diaper kit* with clean diapers, diaper covers, barrier cream, a clean cloth to lay baby down on, and, most importantly, wipes. Make sure all your supplies are easily accessible—not lost at the bottom of your pack.

Whether you are using disposables or cloth diapers, empty feces at an outhouse or dig a hole 15–20 cm deep and bury them. Cloth diapers must be rinsed thoroughly before drying—at least 60 m from any water source. Throw out rinsing water as far away as possible from all water sources (or in the intertidal zone). Do not throw disposable diapers into outhouse toilets; they must be packed out.

Unless you have enough fuel to boil hot water to wash dirty cloth diapers, you may choose to simply rinse, dry, and store used ones.

Footwear

Unless you are hiking trails longer than those in this book, you don't need to buy special hiking shoes for children. For the day hikes and overnights in this book, children will be fine in any comfortable, supportive footwear that is already broken in. It is best if shoes have some ankle support—high-top running shoes and leather ankle boots with good grips have worked well for our children.

Inside shoes or boots, put on a thin pair of synthetic socks to wick moisture and a thicker pair (wool–nylon blend is good) for padding and warmth. A two-layer system helps prevent blisters.

If you are hiking in the summer, sports sandals can be a good choice for day hikes if they have a good sole with serious grip. It is nice to have toes exposed and cool, and quick-drying sports sandals are great if you want to walk on a rocky creekbed.

On very short trails where we expect mud or where there is water to play in at our destination, we will sometimes wear rubber boots. Over long distances, though, rubber boots are impractical. Because of the loose fit, rubbing can quickly cause blisters, and it is easy to slip on uneven ground because the boot does not fit snugly around the foot, and there is no support.

The all-purpose bandana

A bandana is handy as an emergency sun hat (knot the four corners to make a skull cap) and for lots of other things. This is a good item for small children to pack in their own backpacks. Other uses:

- A towel after hand washing.
- A handkerchief.
- A mini-tablecloth.
- A covering over your face when snoozing in the sun.
- An emergency bandage.
- To play hiding-the-object games.
- To tie to a stick as a flag.
- A scarf to keep the neck warm.
- A parachute toy (use some string and a rock).
- The "roof" for a little house made of sticks.

Camp shoes

When we backpack, we always bring a pair of camp shoes in addition to the shoes we hike in. Camp shoes should be lightweight, quick-drying, and easy to slip on and off.

Why have separate shoes for camp? First, extra shoes mean you have something dry as a backup in case hiking shoes get too wet. Second, lighter-weight shoes have less impact on the environment, and when you are in camp tramping down the same area they enable you to leave a lighter footprint. Third, when you are getting in and out of the tent for trips to the bathroom or standing around in your pyjamas washing up at night, you don't want to worry about socks and lacing up a heavy pair of shoes.

Plastic flip-flops or aqua socks (quick-dry neoprene slippers made specifically for use in the water) make excellent camp shoes. On in a flash! Off with a shake or a pull. And they do double duty for protecting feet during water play. Light-weight sports sandals are also good camp shoes.

5

EATING WELL

One cannot think well, love well, sleep well,
if one has not dined well.

—Virginia Woolf

Making sure everyone is eating well is a must when adventuring outdoors with young children. If children don't want to eat what you have
brought, they will emphatically exercise their right of refusal and quickly
become hungry and grumpy. On the other hand, eating well is one of
the joys of hiking and camping.

Getting organized

Planning meals takes time. When preparing for overnight camping,
especially if you are backpacking, make sure you start thinking about
your meals well in advance. For backpacking destinations, we start planning
meals one or two weeks ahead of time, so we can talk about what to
bring, pretest anything we haven't tried before, purchase food items,
repackage them at home so they are smaller and less bulky, and then
have them ready to place in our packs.

We might plan menus one night, shop for groceries another day,
spend an afternoon or evening repackaging food, and then, just before
we leave, add fresh items and pack everything.

Of course, choosing foods for day trips or car camping is easier. Day-
trip snacks are simple to plan and can be purchased at the last minute.
If you are car camping, you have more options for bulky items or per-
ishable foods.

But whether you are doing a wilderness overnight or just a day trip,
it is much easier to spend time preparing food at home in your kitchen
than it is at your destination.

What to bring for day hikes

Even if you think you won't be gone long, don't overlook planning
food for a day hike. We find that even on the shortest walk, we are
all terribly hungry! And snacks can be a very handy motivator. It is

Water break at Sandcut Beach

also very important that you pack adequate food on day hikes in case of emergency. If someone gets hurt and you are delayed, or if you get lost or caught in bad weather, the food in your day pack could be a lifesaver.

On day hikes we like to bring bite-sized foods that fit easily into the hand, like nuts, "gorp" (good ol' raisins and peanuts), crunchy carrot sticks, sliced fruits, sliced bagels, and crackers, along with some quick-energy treats like soft candies or chocolate. Of course, everyone has their own quirky tastes: Sachiko's children will hike very cheerfully when rewarded with Oriental rice crackers, Sachiko likes a bar of Toblerone chocolate, Kari loves a sweet to suck on, and Kari's son Rowan likes to chow down on raw tofu (yes, really!).

Carry plenty of water—at least one litre per adult, less for children. Adults and children alike can easily become dehydrated. Dehydration can contribute to hypothermia, heat stroke, heat cramps, and fatigue. Avoid sugary juices or prepared drinks that don't give the body the same benefit as plain water.

What to bring on overnight or weekend trips

Think about how you will be cooking your food—if you are backpacking and using a backpacking stove, you'll want one-pot meals. If you are near enough to your car to carry in a two-burner Coleman-type stove, you will have more options.

When planning meals, think of each meal as a whole. If you want to have a stir-fry, what do you need to prepare it? In addition to the main ingredients, think about things like cooking oil, spices, sauces, etc.

We make a detailed list of what we will eat each day, itemizing all the ingredients needed for each meal. So for a two-night trip, we'll plan Day 1 breakfast, lunch, and supper, plus day-hike snacks, then the same for Day 2. It is easiest to have a "staples" bag with salt, oil, spices, etc. for easy access at any meal.

Pretest your menu

There is nothing worse than a flop at dinnertime when camping. You can't just open the fridge or head off to the corner store to replace the meal, so pretest your recipes before you go. We never use untried recipes at camp. Adults may eat food they don't like, but our children will not.

When trying out the recipes at home, take note of everything you use to prepare the meal, from cooking oil to tin foil. Be sure to take the item or a replacement on your trip.

Always include snacks for day-hiking and extra emergency food. As with day-hiking, if someone is hurt on the trail or you are delayed for any reason, food can quickly run out.

Avoid butter, fresh meats, eggs, mayonnaise, and mayonnaise-type spreads when planning your meals. If you do decide to eat any of these items on a trip, plan them for the first day and pack them carefully (with a frozen water bottle or in a cooler) so they will not go bad.

Every family will have their favourite foods, but don't be afraid to try something new from time to time! Having something different can add to the pleasure of the adventure. Sachiko's family loves hot pancakes for breakfast, and last season sampled one-pot sushi and one-pot angel-hair pasta with sun-dried tomatoes. Both were great. Kari's family usually makes stir-fries, but was introduced to one-pot chili last season—yum!

We have included some of our favourite recipes at the back of the book, and there are lots of excellent camping cookbooks in the library and in bookstores.

Prepare food as a family

Our children love helping to prepare food before a trip—choosing what to bring, going shopping, measuring out rice, pasta, and other items, premixing ingredients, packaging in zip-lock bags, etc.

We talk about what we could bring and let them give suggestions or say what one special thing they would like to have. When preparing and packaging food, it is fun to set up a family assembly line—someone can measure, another can package, someone else can label, etc.

DRINKS
- Tea
- Juice crystals
- Instant coffee
- Hot chocolate

BREAKFAST FOODS
- Instant oatmeal
- Granola
- Pancake mix (make sure it is the "just-add-water" kind)
- Dried fruits such as apricots, prunes, raisins, apples, pineapples, plums, cherries, pears, peaches
- Bagels and peanut butter

LUNCH
- Jerky
- Salami
- Pepperoni stick
- Hummus (can be purchased in dried form; just add water)
- Peanut butter
- Nuts
- Sunflower and pumpkin seeds
- Fresh vegetables: carrots, cauliflower, broccoli, cucumber
- Fresh fruit: dates, apples, bananas, apricots, etc.
- Breads/crackers: flatbread, pitas, rice crackers
- Hard cheese

BUILDING BLOCKS FOR SUPPERS
- Bulgur (quick-cooking cracked, steamed, and dried wheat)
- Couscous (cracked, steamed, dried wheat, or millet); serve with something crunchy
- Instant Oriental noodles
- Dried pasta
- Dried vegetables
- Instant soups (combine with bulgur, rice, couscous, or noodles)
- Dried fruit
- Instant refried beans or black beans
- Spices, salt, and pepper
- Concentrated tomato paste in a tube (good for pasta and soups)
- Butter or margarine
- Cooking oil

One-pot suppers

For simple, tasty, and nutritious suppers, make any combination of:

1. Carbohydrate or starch (pasta, rice, instant potatoes, couscous, bulgur).
2. Protein (canned chicken, turkey, ham, smoked fish, canned tuna, salmon, crab, cheese, nuts).
3. Vegetable.
4. Sauce/spice flavourings.

Water

How much water to bring? An adult needs a minimum of one litre per day; half that for preschoolers. Calculate using these amounts for your first day of hiking, and then add extra water for emergencies.

It is impractical to carry more than one day's supply of water for several people. On subsequent days, filter, chemically treat (i.e. with chlorine drops), or boil water from water sources on the trail. If you are car camping, you can bring a big refillable water container and keep it in your car.

A small water bottle is a good item for children to pack in their own small packs. If you freeze the bottle the night before, then take it out in the morning, it will be half-thawed when you set out and deliciously cool when you're on the trail. In summer, children will enjoy the treat of a frozen juice box (in addition to water for drinking). If you keep it frozen until you leave, it is like a Popsicle in a box!

Tip: take along baking soda for all-purpose use. It's excellent for scrubbing off pots. It can also be used with water as an emergency rehydration drink; it is very salty.

Feeding infants

BREASTFEEDING

No planning, no preparation—if you are breastfeeding, you simply carry on as you would do at home; breast milk is available any time, anywhere!

We found it very easy to hike and camp while breastfeeding our infants. The only challenge was finding adequate back support and a dry, comfortable place to sit.

A small piece of camping foam is perfect for sitting on and is lightweight for carrying. We cut old camping foam into squares (the whole family uses them for impromptu seats—they are really helpful if you need to sit on wet ground or at a wet picnic table).

For back support, the no-gear option is to locate a large log, a tree trunk, or the side of a bank to lean against. You might not always find the desired backrest when you need it, though. Consider carrying a folding seat—they are lightweight, can be set up anywhere (including in the tent), and provide good support.

BOTTLE-FEEDING

Bottle-feeding is not as easy as breastfeeding, but if done properly can also be successful. Because bacteria is an issue for bottle-fed babies, always use filtered water for sterilizing baby's bottle and for mixing formula. For the same reason, powdered formula is the only safe one for camping.

Rather than having the bother of resterilizing bottles, take bottle-shaped holders and replaceable plastic liners. At mealtime, boil filtered water for five to seven minutes; at the same time boil the nipple and lid. Place boiled water in the plastic liner and add the sterilized nipple and lid. Once your bottle is full of boiled water, it is only a scoop or two away from being ready for a meal. It is not safe to keep mixed formula in a bottle for a day or during the night. Keep the bottle and powdered formula together in a handy spot, and when baby is hungry, scoop the powder into the bottle of water.

For the early-morning feed, place a prepared, sealed bottle of water inside another sealed container at the bottom of one of your sleeping bags. This keeps it at more or less body temperature. When baby wakes, you only have to retrieve the formula powder to make it ready. Never keep formula in the tent. Store it with other food out of reach of animals.

Food management and animals
- Never leave food unattended!
- Hang all food in a bag suspended from a tree or pole, or store it in hard-sided tight-lidded containers. In some backcountry sites, bear wires are available for hanging food, while other sites may have bear-proof caches.
- Never store food or eat food in your tent.
- Pack out all uneaten food and food waste; don't dispose of it in the wild.
- Wash dirty dishes promptly.
- Keep a clean camp.
- To avoid odour-tainting your pack, clothing, and gear, store scented articles in sealed plastic bags.
(Adapted from *Olympic National Wilderness Trip Planner*)

Food should be hung at least 3 metres off the ground, and 1.5 metres out from the tree trunk

Hot Breakfast in the Rain

It has rained all night. We slept to the gentle tapping on the tent roof, and now, in the morning, it is still falling. Elena, Marin, and I snuggle in our sleeping bags, breathing in the fresh, humid air.

Through the open tent door, we see Joseph already under the tarp, rummaging in the food bag. He promises banana-raisin pancakes!

We come to life—wiggling out of bed, pulling on sweaters, and reaching for our boots. We perch on a bleached log under the tarp—a dry breakfast bench looking out at the sea and sky, and the beach with its big, exposed tide pools.

Soon there are sizzles from the small frying pan and the sweet smell of batter and ripe banana. We laugh and talk about what we will do today. The hot pancakes are steaming and there is even maple syrup!

6

PACKING

On a long journey,
even a straw seems heavy.

—Spanish proverb

Packing well means carrying what you have most efficiently. This is particularly important when, in addition to shouldering a heavy pack, a parent needs to hold a toddler's hand or catch up with a preschooler running too far ahead on the trail.

Getting ready for an overnight trip

The first step in packing for an overnight trip is to gather up all the gear, food, clothes, etc. that you have identified on your checklists. Usually you will have what looks like a big mess—a kitchen table piled with food bags, and several small heaps of clothes, cooking pots, flashlights, and first-aid kit items lying on the floor. Now you need a large space where you can spread out! We use the living room or, if it is a nice sunny day, the backyard.

Start with triage: separate items that are "wants" from those that are "needs." Pack extras later, if you have room. Remove any unnecessary packaging so that you are bringing only what you really need. Zip-lock bags are fabulous for this.

Compartmentalize small same-category items, like first-aid supplies and cooking utensils, for easy retrieval by placing them into a stuff sack or a plastic bag. Label it if it is not see-through. Check off items as you pack them. Once you have packed things, it is a real hassle trying to take inventory again.

If you are not backpacking, you can load your gear into almost anything, but remember that carrying uncomfortable loads can be agony—even for a short trip. Try to put everything into a proper carrying bag or pack. It is much easier to carry one or two bags than 20 miscellaneous containers and sacks.

Give yourself enough time. Don't underestimate how long packing can take! We find that for a backpacking trip, we need at least a half-day just to pack. Avoid leaving things too late—it is *not* fun starting off on a trip when you have been up until 2 a.m. packing, the children are awake at 6:30, and you have a two-hour drive and then a two-hour hike ahead of you.

With car camping, you can get away with throwing everything together in a couple of hours. But wouldn't it be less stressful to have everything ready the night before and be able to leave on time, with no last-minute running around?

Packing a backpack

If you are backpacking to your destination, packing requires more care. Everything must be kept dry, space must be used efficiently, and the load must be manageable and well balanced.

If you have backpacked without children, keep in mind that on trips with little ones, the load will be heavier than on previous adults-only hikes (because you are carrying all their stuff as well as your own—including bulky things like diapers).

Anything that needs to stay dry should be placed in bags before going into the pack. We pack each person's clothes in a plastic grocery bag—rolling clothes compresses them better—and we label the bag with a permanent marker. This keeps clothes dry if the pack gets wet, and makes sorting out whose clothes are where much easier. In addition to our individual clothing bags, we put all our pyjamas into a separate bag—that way we don't have to rummage through individual bags at night. This is especially helpful on the first night after a long day.

Wherever possible, nest smaller items inside larger ones and nest flexible items inside hard-sided things (e.g., put zip-lock bags of dry ingredients inside hard-sided pots), so you don't have any empty "pockets" in the pack that are not serving a purpose.

The gathering stage usually looks like a big mess

How to balance the load

Goal: To be able to walk comfortably, without too much pressure on the neck, back, hips, or shoulders.

How to achieve it: Keep the pack's centre of gravity as close as possible to your own, and balance weight evenly.

Put heavier items (tent, stove, pots, food, extra water, etc.) at the top between your shoulder blades, and as close to your back as possible. This keeps the heavy items close to your centre of gravity and transfers weight to the pack's frame so that it can be supported by your hips.

Place medium-weight items (clothes, raingear) in the middle of the pack. Keep light items (sleeping bag, sleeping pads) at the bottom (on external-frame packs, you can tie sleeping gear outside the pack at the bottom).

Place small related items together in small bags inside your pack. It is much easier to find the red stuff sack with the pens and papers in it than it is to grope around the bottom of your pack for a pen.

Put everything you need handy into accessible pockets, or in the lid of the pack where they are easiest to reach (toilet paper, map, hat, sunscreen, snack, first aid, etc.) We have standard places we keep small items so that we always know where they are.

Once your pack is fully loaded, test it out. It's much easier to make adjustments at home than it is after you develop an aching shoulder and a sore back on the trail.

Keeping your pack dry

Always carry a garbage bag large enough to go over your entire pack in case of heavy rain. It weighs nothing and takes up very little space, but could make the difference between all your gear being wet or dry.

If you plan to carry a sleeping bag outside your pack, line your stuff sack with a garbage bag. Most stuff sacks are *not* waterproof.

Water bottles can leak and they can also get wet simply from condensation. Screw them closed tightly and wrap them in a plastic bag. Pack water upright if possible and in a separate compartment away from the camera, dry clothes, etc.

Kari lost a camera once when her mother, an inexperienced hiker at the time, packed her water bottle next to it. The bottle leaked—just a little—and the camera was ruined.

Children's backpacks

Children often love to have their own tiny pack to bring along so they can feel they are contributing to the trip. Make sure it fits, and is not too large.

Toddlers can't carry much, even for a short time, but older children might carry a small pack for an entire hike. We purposely limit the contents of our children's packs so they are mostly empty because when they decide they *don't* want to carry the pack anymore, guess what? We have to find somewhere to stuff it—inside our own packs.

Possible items for a child's backpack:

- Survival items (see Chapter 9)
- Bandana
- Tiny books
- Pen and paper
- A few snacks
- Flashlight
- Map (maybe one they have drawn)

Three-year-old Marin and her backpack

Pack going-home outfits

For multi-day trips, we always pack a duffel bag full of clean, non-hiking clothes, which we leave in the car at the trailhead. After several days in the wild, it is so nice to be able to change your clothes and feel somewhat clean before heading home. These dry clothes are a good backup in case of emergency as well. If you become soaked on the hike out, having easy-access dry clothing at the trailhead will help everyone warm up quickly.

7

NO-TRACE TRAIL ETHICS

I believe a leaf of grass is no less
than the journey-work of the stars.

—Walt Whitman

One of the reasons we love to go outdoor adventuring is to experience the gift of nature's beauty, or as Whitman puts it so poetically, the "journey-work of the stars." Seeing litter or the remnants of someone else's camp lying around, or a meadow that has been criss-crossed and eroded by unnecessary trails, spoils the aesthetic experience. More importantly, careless practices damage the delicate balance of the natural environment, sometimes permanently.

A simple mantra: "Leave no trace. Leave no trace. Leave no trace." We want to leave the wild beautiful and undisturbed.

Children are naturally protective and caring of their environment. This is a wonderful age to teach no-trace ethics. Lead by example and explain the *why* behind what you do.

Keep to the trail

The trail is there so that environmental impact will be contained to the trail path itself. Walking off the trail damages fragile habitat. Shortcutting creates more areas of erosion, destroys ground cover, can contribute to run-off problems if a shortcut becomes a channel for water run-off, and can destroy animal habitats and homes.

If you see an unauthorized shortcut, you can help prevent further damage by throwing some brush across it, or obstructing it with a log.

If the trail is single-file only, walk single-file, in the middle of the trail. Try to avoid going off-trail around muddy sections if you can (this just widens the trail and increases the impact).

Leave what you find

Although it might be fun to build a fort or some other structure, in the spirit of "Leave No Trace," don't alter the found environment. Enjoy examining rocks, plants, and other objects, but leave them as you find them.

A Leaf is a Home

One spring day, four-year-old Rowan, Kari, and Kari's mother (who had just moved west) were walking in Francis/King Park when Rowan noticed that his grandma was collecting leaves.

"Grandma, those are slug *habitats*."

Abashed, she put them back, then laughed and said, "I didn't know the word 'habitat' until I was in university." She was proud of her grandson's care for the environment.

On a practical note, when children know that they can't collect things, you won't end up with them begging you to help them carry endless handfuls of treasure!

Camp on durable surfaces

We all like to find a beautiful spot to set up our tent. But idyllic as camping in the middle of the meadow may seem, first ask yourself if you are choosing a site where you will have the least impact. As a rule, don't tent in fragile meadows. Always use existing sites where possible. Don't dig, level, or sweep away the ground for your comfort; if there are uncomfortable stones, pine cones, sticks, etc., pick them up and set them aside. When you leave, scatter them back over the site.

Remember that fallen logs are some of the richest habitats in the woods. Check to see if anything is living in, under, or on a log before moving it.

Choose well-drained or sandy spots wherever possible, and make sure you are at least 60 m away from any water source.

Dispose of trash properly

Pack it in, pack it out. Every adult in our group always carries a zip-lock bag in a handy place (an outer pack pocket, a fanny pack, or stuffed into a jacket pocket). Food wrappers, kleenex, leftover food, and anyone else's litter we find goes into the zip-lock. When hiking with babies, we carry a special bag for packing out soiled diapers.

When Nature calls

Three-year-old Elena announces with great urgency, "I need to go pee!" No problem. A nicely constructed provincial park privy is just a step away. "This is an outhouse," says Mama. "A little house that has a toilet in it. You can go pee in there." She nods agreeably.

However, as the door creaks open on its rusty hinge, Elena screws up her face and declares: "No ... It smells BAD!"

"It will only take a minute. Mama will hold your nose and you won't smell anything."

"No ... I don't want to! I don't want to! No!!!" She *refuses* to go in.

GENERAL RULES

Take advantage of every possibility to use a toilet before you no longer have access to them. Have everyone stop if there is an outhouse at the trailhead or along the trail, regardless of whether they think they need to go or not. If and when no outhouse is available or when your children refuse to use it, you have limited options and must observe these general rules:

- *Make sure you are at least 60 m from any water source* (creek, stream, ocean, etc.), and from trails or campsites.
- *Bury solid waste in a hole*—a primitive latrine. Why? To minimize the risk of water pollution and spread of giardia, to minimize the chance of people or animals finding the waste, and to maximize rapid decomposition.

While in most situations you should use a hole, properly dealing with solid waste depends somewhat on geography. At a beach, you should be in the intertidal zone, where the rising tide will carry the

---

Digging a latrine

- Use a stick or trowel to **dig a hole 15-20 cm deep** (the depth at which micro-organisms will work on breaking down human waste).
- After you've done the job, use the trowel or a stick to **mix soil with waste** (this speeds decomposition).
- **Cover with topsoil** to camouflage the surface.

Have your child help you dig the hole (providing you have enough lead time!) and cover it afterwards.
Explain why you need to bury the waste. Three-year-old Elena, who refused to use a smelly outhouse, was fascinated by the whole process and surprisingly enthusiastic about digging and burying. You never know!

waste away (this may be too disconcerting for some, since there is little privacy there—if so, follow the 60-m rule). In the high alpine zone, where flora is very fragile, you should not dig a hole. Ideally all waste should be carried out of alpine areas because the coldness slows decomposition. However, if that is not possible, be discreet and try to cover waste with a rock or piece of moss.

- Trowel (a plastic gardening trowel is perfect). Keep it wrapped in a plastic bag; it will be difficult to get it properly clean.
- Individual zip-lock bags with toilet paper—one for each adult, and one for children carrying day packs. We pre-rip the paper into lengths of several squares for easier access in a hurry.
- One large zip-lock bag for soiled paper.
- Zip-lock bag with wet wipes, for washing hands.

PACK OUT TOILET PAPER
All used toilet paper goes into the large zip-lock bag. Back at the trailhead, empty the contents into the outhouse or, better yet, empty it at home. Don't throw the zip-lock bag in the outhouse toilet; *it will not decompose.* Take it home, wash and rinse it in your toilet, rinse with bleach solution, and then put it in your regular garbage—the cycle of care for the wild includes proper garbage disposal. Don't burn toilet paper! Entire forests have been destroyed by this practice.

Feminine hygiene
On overnight trips, especially to backpack wilderness sites, bring a few sheets of folded aluminum foil, several aspirins, and a zip-lock bag for packing out tampons or pads. Place tampons or pads on the foil, scatter crushed aspirins over top, and wrap with foil. This will minimize odour—especially important in areas where bears may be present. Place the foil package in a zip-lock bag. Store up high in a bear-proof bag while at camp.

Minimize campfire impact
Many of us may remember childhood camping trips where a campfire was *de rigeur.* The smell of the wood burning, the sound of the fire crackling, the glow of the sparks against the night sky, the warmth emanating from the embers ... But fires do have an impact, and it can be long-lasting. In some areas, fires are not permitted. Even if they are, treat fires as a luxury, and if you have one, ensure a minimum impact on the environment.

How do you leave no trace?
- Keep your fire small.
- Never build a fire on the top layer of organic soil—it is highly flammable and can smoulder underground for weeks.
- Locate a good source of mineral soil (like sand) in an area that doesn't require excavation. Collect the mineral soil and carry it to your fire site. A stuff sack works well.
- Lay the soil on bare ground, create a 20-cm-high mound and flatten off the top (the mound insulates the ground below from the fire). Make sure the mound is larger than the fire you plan to have, so it will contain the fire's spread.
- Build the fire on top of the mound.
- On beaches, light fires on shingle rocks and sand so no scars are left, and burn all wood completely.
- When the fire is burned to white ash and the ashes are cold, stir through the embers to ensure it's out.
- Douse fire with water.
- You should leave no sign of your fire; use a stick to disperse ash and remaining sticks, and scatter signs of your presence.

FIRE-BUILDING DON'TS
- Don't use damp stones for a fire ring; they can explode with heat.
- Don't build a fire against a large rock—the blackened mark from burning the rock will scar the rock for longer than your lifetime.
- Don't remove any wood from living trees! Use only fallen wood. Collect only what you need.
- Don't burn toxic materials such as plastic. When in doubt, just don't.

8

HOME AWAY FROM HOME

Now I see the secret of the making of the best persons.
It is to grow in the open air and to eat and sleep with the earth.

—Walt Whitman

Lying under the brilliance of the night sky and speculating about the nature of the universe. Hearing surf crash all night long from the cozy nest of a sleeping bag. Sitting on a warm rock and sharing food in the afternoon sun. Looking out of the tent door in the morning (even after a restless night with a baby!) to see pale pink light on the water. These are the pleasures of making a home in the wild for a night or two.

Whether at a more established walk-in tent site or at a wilderness site, we want to take care to be gentle with our surroundings, and at the same time, make our temporary home comfortable, practical, and safe.

As a rule of thumb, choose a well-drained or sandy spot for your camp whenever possible and stay out of fragile meadows. Use existing sites when possible so you do not damage ground cover. Make sure you are at least 60 m from any water source. Identify where you will get water, and where you will be able to go to the bathroom.

Setting up camp

Depending on the number of adults in your group and the age of your small children, this can be easy or quite challenging. With just two adults, and babies or toddlers who require a parent's constant supervision, one person is going to end up doing most of the set-up, while the other parent entertains, feeds, carries, etc.

It helps to have a tent that can be easily set up by one person (most of the newer-model dome tents fit the bill). Make sure you know how to put up your tent and have gone through a test drive at home.

Toddlers want to help, even if they are seldom efficient. They love to be included, and can carry small loads or help pass out supplies (like tent stakes).

Our older children are now past the toddler years and are enthusiastic, cheerful assistants. With a little patience on our part, they are very helpful with unpacking the gear, picking out and testing a tent spot, laying down the groundsheet, pushing in the tent stakes, and putting poles into the right slots and raising the tent. Setting up camp is a wonderful learning opportunity for them and a teachable moment for us.

Establishing a boundary

Decide on a boundary for your campsite. You can mark the bounds with visual landmarks or natural objects—preschoolers will enjoy setting the bounds with you. Tell them they can play within the boundary, but can't go farther without an adult.

On beaches where driftwood is plentiful, create a "nest" of driftwood fences to contain toddlers. Return the logs to their original spots when you break camp.

Siting your tent

Look around carefully before siting your tent. Make sure you are on fairly level ground, and that the ground is high enough to ensure it will be dry. For minimum impact look for sand, dry grasses, or other surfaces where you will not crush fragile plant life.

Where would your site be if there was run-off from a heavy rain? When beach camping, always consult a tide table before pitching your tent. Also think about getting out of the tent to go to the toilet at night, possibly in the dark. Is the terrain manageable? When the weather looks iffy, set up your tent in the shelter of a tree if possible, to help keep wind and rain away.

To test out your spot, spread out your groundsheet or just lie on the ground. Kids love doing this! You'll find out which end of the tent site is higher and whether or not there are any roots or stones that would be uncomfortable to sleep on. Doing this now is *much* easier than waiting until after the tent is up, everyone is in their sleeping bags, it is dark, and someone discovers they have something jabbing into their back! If there is an incline, set things up so your head is at the higher end.

Setting up your tent

If the tent fly touches the tent, water can come inside at the contact points. Make sure your fly is pulled taut and well away from the walls of your tent (remember—the fly will droop when wet and consequently come closer to the tent).

We always set up our tent soon after arrival and at the same time get everything ready for night (even if it's morning when we arrive). Weather can change quickly, and it is not easy setting up camp in a panic if it

9

Seeing in the dark

We bring strips of Velcroed fluorescent safety tape in our tent bag, and wrap tapes around the guy lines once the tent is up. At dusk and at night, these glow in the dark and prevent tripping on tent ropes.

Sticky fluorescent tape can also be used to mark all kinds of small things like flashlights—no more groping around for them in the dark.

---

starts to rain or as dusk falls and it is difficult to see well.

After putting up the tent, lay out sleeping pads, arrange sleeping bags, and put your bag of nighttime clothes in the tent. We also make sure we have a flashlight, matches, roll of toilet paper, and dry raingear inside the tent—many mornings we have woken up to a rainstorm and been thankful that matches and raingear were in the tent!

Two rules for tents: no wet items inside, and no eating inside (any food, even crumbs, can attract unwanted animals).

Creating a comfy bed

Years ago, we designed a method for creating a comfortable bed in our tent. We have adapted it over the years, but the essentials stay the same.

It starts with a *dry under-layer*—if your tent is not waterproof, this is where a groundsheet will come in handy (make sure it is underneath the tent). Over that we place a *barrier layer* such as a camping mattress. This not only adds comfort, it also traps cold away from the sleeping bodies above. Over this we place the *insulating layer*—our sleeping bags—and, depending on how cold it is, we sometimes throw a fleece blanket over top. Remember that cold can often come from the bottom, not the top. If you are cold in the night, try putting an extra blanket or sweater under your hips and chest.

We used to place our camping mats lengthwise so they would fit underneath the footprint of each sleeping bag. But when people moved around at night, we'd end up with a gap—sometimes a chasm—between the two mats, and one of us would be sleeping on, over, or in the gap. Now we place our sleeping mats horizontally, so one sits underneath everyone's head/shoulders, another is in the middle, and a third (if needed) is at the feet. This eliminates the gap problem.

Tip: When you arrive, and in the mornings, unzip sleeping bags and open them for a few minutes to air them out. Then shake them to fluff the loft—this will keep your bag warmer.

- Area, trail route planned, destination.
- Vehicle info (licence number, make, model).
- Equipment and supplies taken.

Always carry the "Ten Essentials"

In the 1930s, the Mountaineers (a Seattle-based organization) coined the term "The Ten Essentials" for a list of safety items that you should have at all times, whether day hiking or backpacking. In addition to the Ten Essentials, we recommend carrying:

- Wire or duct tape (for repairs).
- Bandana (can be used as a makeshift sling, hat, or washcloth).

Wear bright-coloured clothing for easy visibility

Wearing bright-coloured clothes makes it easier to keep track of everyone in the group. If the worst happens and someone is lost, bright colours will make it easier for rescuers to find the lost person.

Stay on the trail and stay together

Never hike off-trail unless you have high-level orienteering and wilderness survival skills. Teach your children that no one hikes alone. If children want to run ahead, they must be with an adult or must stop at an agreed-upon landmark and wait for the group to catch up.

Never drink unpurified water

According to the U.S. Centers for Disease Control, no surface water in the world can be guaranteed free of the *giardia lamblia* parasite. *Giardia* is a waterborne disease and can be present even in the most pristine-looking wilderness streams. The risk is not worth it. Symptoms include cramping, serious diarrhea, headache, low-grade fever, and appetite loss lasting up to three weeks and sometimes becoming chronic and lasting for years.

Consult tide tables and know terrain when beach hiking

Rising tides can trap you below unpassable cliffs, treacherous headlands can be impossible to hike, and powerful waves can throw giant logs right into your path. Always carry a detailed map and a tide chart (which you must know how to use) if you intend to beach hike.

Beware of headland trails. These are trails that lead from the beach over headland cliffs. Usually they are steep and muddy and very challenging—too difficult to attempt with young children.

The Ten Essentials: always carry these for safety

1. **Water.** We need at least one litre per day per person for survival and should have about three litres per day. Always carry adequate water (and some extra) on day hikes. Never depend on finding water on the trail—it is a dangerous practice to drink untreated water anywhere; *giardia* is present even in the most pristine backcountry, and much surface water is affected by contaminants. For backpacking trips, carry bottled water as well as a way to purify more on the trail (for short trips, this is usually a stove and fuel for boiling water, or chlorine or iodine purification tablets).

2. **Emergency Food.** Always bring more food than you think you will need. It's easier than you think to be out much longer than planned—miscalculating distance, sustaining an unexpected injury, etc. You may need that extra food to give everyone the energy they need to get back safely.

3. **Raingear and extra clothing.** No matter what the forecast says, be prepared. Countless times we have set off on what looked like a perfect, sunny, warm, cloudless day. And guess what? An hour later, the sky darkened, a wind whipped up, and rain began to spatter. Sometimes just moving from open trail into heavy forest is enough to warrant pulling on a sweater or pants. Bring rain and wind clothes, sweaters, and warm pants and a warm hat for each family member.

4. **First-aid supplies.** Carry a well-prepared first-aid kit (see checklist at the back of the book) and make sure you know how to use everything you bring. Invest time in a basic first-aid class.

5. **Army knife or multi-purpose tool.** This is the most useful tool you can carry, in addition to being helpful at snack time.

6. **Map.** Don't leave home without the best map you can get; obtain a topographic map whenever possible. For longer hikes or overnights, a detailed map of your route is crucial to help you find water, get reoriented, or find an emergency exit route.

7. **Compass.** If you don't know how to use a compass, make time to learn how. If you are lost, the best map in the world is useless unless you know how to orient yourself.

8. **Fire starter and matches.** Use these to build a fire for warmth or to signal for help (you need both—you can't light fire starter without matches).

9. **Flashlight and extra bulbs/batteries.** Use these to find your way in the dark or for signalling for help.

10. **A large orange plastic bag for each person in the group.** This can be an emergency shelter, make-do raingear, or a signalling device. You can also buy a bright orange "survival bag" for less than five dollars at outdoor stores. It is large enough to be a sleeping sack for an adult and is made of durable three-mm polyethylene.

Think ahead

- Eat before you are very hungry.
- Rest before you are exhausted.
- Get warmer clothes on before you are really cold.
- Regularly check children's warmth, especially hands, cheeks, and back of the neck. Children won't always tell you when they are starting to get cold.

Never rely on cellphones

Many fall into the trap of thinking that carrying a cellphone means you don't have to be prepared for an emergency. Cellphone coverage is hit and miss. There is no guarantee that your phone will be in range (most of our overnight destinations are outside of cell coverage).

You may need to act very quickly if there is an injury, and a cellphone is no substitute for first-aid supplies and know-how. Follow all the guidelines for safety preparedness we have outlined here.

Carry adequate first-aid supplies

Always carry a fully stocked first-aid kit, both for day hikes and on overnights. When you return from a trip, make it part of your routine to replace anything that you have used.

Your supplies should include skin-care products (sunscreen, burn treatment, insect repellent, blister pads), antiseptic solution and antibiotic ointment, medications (for pain relief, skin rashes, allergies, diarrhea, poison, sore throat, etc.), and basic equipment like tweezers, scissors, safety pins, etc.

We have included a detailed first-aid supply checklist and a quick reference for common first-aid situations (prevention, symptoms, and treatment) at the back of the book.

Teach your children trail safety

Parents are sometimes hesitant to talk to their children about what might happen if a child became lost or separated from their group, for fear of scaring the child.

None of us like to think of our child lost and alone in the wilderness, and we don't expect it to happen. But the fact is that anyone can become lost (see Hug-A-Tree info box). Children need to know what to do if they become separated from you, and taking the time to educate your children may be a lifesaving gift for them.

If you think you're lost, hug a tree or find a "house" where you will wait.
Discuss how it might be scary to be alone and lost. Suggest that they
find a rock, a log, or a tree that is out in the open and pretend it's their
"house." Hugging a tree or other object and even talking to it can be
calming and it may also prevent panic.

It's very important to stay in one place. Reassure them that when you
notice they are missing, you will bring friends to look for them where
you last saw them, so it is important for them to stay where they are.
Tell them that if they try to find you, they may become more lost, and
that will make it harder to find them. Talk about how it can be hard to
wait for a long time, but reiterate that you will be searching for them
and you won't stop until you find them. Reinforce again that it is important for them to stay where they are and wait, so you will be able to
find them faster.

Blow your whistle instead of yelling for help. If your children are old
enough to know how to blow a whistle, give them their very own and
teach them the universal distress signal (three short "tweets"). Teach
them to blow the whistle as hard as they can rather than trying to
shout (the whistle can be heard from much farther away, while yelling will tire them out and use precious energy). Clapping is also a
good way to communicate, and the sound travels much better than
human voices.

Make sure you are easy to see. Suggest they stay in the open if possible.
If you have prepared them well, and they are carrying survival items,

Hug-A-Tree-and-Survive Program

Tragically, a young boy in California died when he was separated from his
brothers while on a popular nature trail only half a mile from the family's
campsite, in spite of a three-day search by 400 searchers, including 200 Marines.

The Hug-A-Tree-and-Survive program was founded to help prevent such a
tragedy from occurring again, and was specifically designed to teach survival
principles to children aged 5–12.

Hug-A-Tree recommends that children always carry a bright garbage bag
(pre-cut with a hole for the face, so they can put it over their head and keep
dry and warm) and a whistle.

See **gpsar.org/hugatree.html** for the sobering story of nine-year-old
Jimmy Beveridge and more survival suggestions to share with your children.

Contents of a Kids' Kit of survival items

Water bottle and snacks.

Lightstick. Cost: under $5. Look for the 12-hour kind, found in outdoor stores. They are bright, don't need batteries, and can provide a sense of assurance to a child who is waiting. Tell your child: "If you snap this stick and shake it, it will be light for a long time and you can use it at night while you are waiting for us. It loses its light little by little, but it will stay bright for a long time if you wait to use it until it is dark."

Emergency blanket. Cost: about $5 in outdoor stores. The "Space" brand of emergency blanket is tiny—small enough to fit in a pocket; it is waterproof, windproof, and reflects body heat to provide warmth. Note: These are very hard to get out of the store packaging—parents should remove them carefully, keeping them folded, and put into a zip-lock bag before including in the kit. Tell your child: "This will keep you warm and dry while you wait for us. You can wrap it all around you, but don't put it over your face. We can't open it up right now, because we can't fold it back this small again."

Rescue whistle. Cost: minimal. Tell your child: "If you get lost, blow three tweets on the whistle. Then wait. Then blow three tweets again. This signal lets everyone know you need help. We can hear a whistle much better than we can hear your voice. Trying to yell will tire you out."

Orange garbage bag (with hole cut out for the head).
Cost: minimal. Tell your child: "This is a very bright colour and will help people find you. You can wave it, or attach it to a stick and wave it like a flag, or hang it from a tree. If you rest, put it out flat beside you. If it is raining, you can put it over your head like a rain poncho [make sure they know to keep their head out]. We will look for it because we know you have it and it will be a signal for us to look for."

Signal mirror. Cost: about $10. Small, plastic, highly reflective mirror. Tell your child: "This mirror looks ordinary, but you can use it to reflect sunlight and then we can see the light signal from very far away." To practise this at home, try putting paper plates on trees in the backyard and practise reflecting light onto the targets. Caution: Never direct a light beam into someone's eyes.

Personal-care items. Can include small package of tissues, some small bandages, and some wet wipes. These are intended to add a sense of preparedness for the child. Tell your child: "You can use the tissues if you need to go to the bathroom and the bandages and wipes in case you have a cut or scrape."

Adapted from http://www.mpioutdoors.com/can.htm

they can open out a bright orange garbage bag or even wrap themselves in it (see Hug-A-Tree box in this chapter).

No one will be angry at you. Children may be afraid parents will be angry with them. If they know you will be understanding and loving, they will be less frightened, less likely to panic, and will work harder to be found.

Ensure your children have their own emergency gear

At the very least, older children should carry their own small packs, with a whistle, a large orange garbage bag, water, and some snacks. Better yet, take the time to put together a "Kids' Kit" of survival items, and have them carry their own warm clothing in their packs.

A grandfather in the U.S. developed the Kids' Kit as a way to teach and prepare his grandson for trail safety. Together with your child, you prepare a kit of safety items especially for your child that she will carry herself in her own backpack or fanny pack. As you work together creating the kit, you have a great opportunity to discuss how to use the items to stay safe. The kit includes a water bottle, lightstick, whistle, emergency blanket, orange garbage bag, mirror, a package of tissues, and wet wipes.

Wildlife

Many people who have grown up in urban areas and have had little first-hand knowledge of the wild while growing up are nervous about meeting wildlife. "What about bears?" they ask. "Is it safe?"

Both of us have lived and hiked in areas rich in wildlife for much of our lives. As with anything else, a little knowledge goes a long way. We know that statistically we have a much greater chance of being injured by a car while crossing the street on any given day in a city than of being attacked by an animal while on the trail.

For the most part, wild animals keep to themselves and want as little to do with humans as possible. Being familiar with their habits can help us prevent an unwanted encounter and help us know what to do should one occur.

PREVENTING UNWELCOME WILDLIFE ENCOUNTERS

- Speak in conversational tones and use "bear bells" to gently signal your approach along the trail.
- Keep children in the middle of your group, never out front or in the rear on their own.
- Don't approach animals, especially young animals. Mothers are likely to attack if they think people are a threat to their young.

- Never, never feed wild animals. This disrupts the natural order of things. Wild animals who become used to food from humans can become aggressive and lose their natural fear of humans.
- Control food odours and minimize use of scented items; never store food in your tent or out in the open—keep it in sealed containers.
- Don't use scented lip balms. Store toothpaste, sunscreen, insect repellent, etc., as though they are food.

COUGARS

Cougars may be encountered at some of the destinations in this book, although it is unlikely: cougars are usually solitary and nocturnal. They hunt prey by stalking and rushing or by pouncing from trees or overhangs. Though sightings are rare, cougars can be very dangerous, especially to children and small adults. If you come across cougar scat or prints, leave the area immediately. If you meet a cougar, *remember that cougars are intimidated by height*:

- Get small children off the ground immediately, possibly onto your shoulders.
- Try to make yourself appear as big and threatening as possible (hold something over your head, like gear or branches; spread your jacket like wings to look wider).
- Do *not* crouch or play dead.
- Stay calm; don't yell or make movements that might startle the animal.
- Stand your ground; speak firmly and constantly.
- Back away slowly, facing cougar and throwing stones or sticks at it.
- If it attacks, fight back; hit it on the head; try to stay on your feet.

BEARS

Bears may be encountered at some of the destinations in this book. Bears usually go out of their way to avoid humans. They only attack when startled or if trying to protect their cubs. If you make enough noise, bears usually retreat rather than confront people. However, bears can run very fast and are adept at climbing trees. Never get between a bear and her cubs; this is a common cause of attack. If you meet a bear:

- Be quiet; speak in a low voice (loud talk or screams may be perceived as a threat and will make the bear more aggressive).
- Don't run, yell, or startle the bear.
- Back away, without turning your back.

- *Only if caught off-guard*, play dead: lie face down, curl into a ball, lock hands behind head, keep arms as close to body as possible. This protects vital organs, face, and neck.
- If bear leaves, do not move for a while.

RACCOONS

Raccoons are a pest rather than a danger and will brazenly tear apart any kind of gear. Don't leave *anything* unattended. Hang what you can. Store anything else in your tent. Although they are unafraid of humans and normally don't attack, they can be surly. Keep your camp clean.

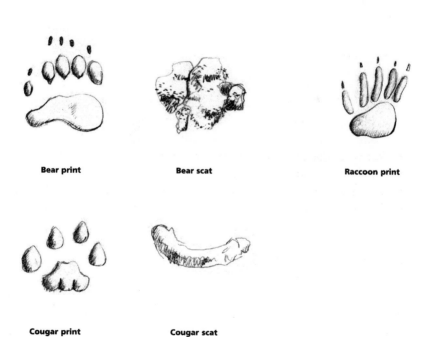

Bear print **Bear scat** **Raccoon print**

Cougar print **Cougar scat**

10

ON THE ROAD

Cheerful company shortens the journey.

–German proverb

With young children, sometimes the hardest part about an outdoor adventure is just getting there. Long periods of time confined by a five-point harness in a car seat are no child's idea of fun. And when little ones aren't happy, no one's happy. The memory of a young child whining and complaining (or screaming!) can make any parent think twice about going away.

Timing your trip

Think carefully about your children and what will best suit their routine and temperaments.

With babies, plan to take longer than expected to accommodate nursing or bottle-feeding and diaper changes. If you are blessed with a baby who doesn't like sleeping in the car (we've been there!), try leaving soon after baby wakes up. With toddlers, try to have driving times coincide with established nap times.

Plan to arrive at your destination early. Arriving at mealtimes or too close to dark can be disastrous, unless you have planned ahead. If you will be hiking in to a campsite from a trailhead, arrive early enough in the day that you will have ample time to unload all your gear, get yourselves organized, and have plenty of time for the hike, for the set-up at camp, and for a meal before dusk.

Strategies for long drives

For long trips to overnight destinations, Sachiko's family leaves very early in the morning. The children go to bed already dressed in comfy, loose, day clothes. They are groggy and barely stir as they are sleepily buckled into car seats in the faint early-morning light. As a two-year-old, Marin sometimes would cry when moved from bed to car, but she was usually fast asleep within 10 minutes once the car started moving.

A sunny knoll at John Dean Park

The benefits? Usually the children sleep soundly for several hours (all the way from Victoria to Courtenay on one trip). Roads are quiet and driving is less stressful in the early hours. When they arrive at the destination, the girls are rested and energetic, and ready for a hike!

Kari's son Rowan hardly ever sleeps in a car, so her family plans trips between meals so that everyone is well fed and comfortable for the drive. Rowan enjoys listening to books on tape and is eager to get out and hike at the end of the journey.

Pack snacks and easy-to-eat meals

Drinks and healthy snacks can stretch the time between breakfast and lunch or lunch and dinner. If you know you are going to arrive around mealtime, plan a meal that can be eaten out of a handy bag—sandwiches, snack bars, bottled drinks, fruit. Children can eat quickly, leaving time for parents to set up camp or to get the hiking underway. Children enjoy preparing their own snack bag and water bottle the night before.

Avoid all sugary snacks! Children on sugar will find it very hard to sit in a car—make sure snacks are high in nutrition, low in sugar.

Drink water. It's a healthier choice than sugared juice and pop, which make children need to pee sooner and more often.

Make sure children are comfortable

Don't overlook the effect of sun in your children's eyes or of tight, uncomfortable clothing on their mood. We keep two large, folded pieces of cardboard in the back of the car that we use to shield the sun when it's too hot or bright. Store-bought window shades would also do the trick, or you could improvise with a draped towel or blanket. We always keep a pillow and light blanket handy for each child.

Our children travel in loose, stretchy clothing like sweatpants, and take off their shoes in the car. Be careful if you put sleepy children in the car with no shoes! Sachiko's family forgot to bring Elena's hiking boots on one trip and she had to use sandals—which, fortunately, had been packed in the "going-home clothes" bag.

Plan for breaks en route

Know your children's limits when it comes to sitting for long periods. Build in time for breaks when everyone can get out and enjoy fresh air and a short walk or run around.

Stop where there are toilet facilities, such as a public beach or playground. If you are travelling over a mealtime, break at a place where you can have a pleasant picnic.

Best in-car snacks

Healthy, easy clean-up, not very sticky or messy to eat:
- Raisins
- Nuts
- Pretzels
- Dry cereal, like Cheerios
- Cheese cubes
- Cold quesadillas, cut into triangles
- Dried fruit
- Cut-up apples
- Carrot and cucumber sticks
- Drinks from sippy cups or bottles with straws

Pit stops are necessary, but too many of them can make the trip overly long. Make sure toddlers and older children go to the bathroom before the trip starts. It can be helpful to tell children where you are going to stop, so that they can focus on that destination as a break.

Keeping little ones happy

Car travel can be boring and frustrating for babies in back-facing car seats; Sachiko's infant daughter hated it. Some ideas:
- Colourful pictures that you can tape to the seat back and change every so often.
- Rattles and music-makers.
- A few pieces of mega-blocks.
- Interlocking "links" that can make a chain, from which you can hang a variety of things.
- Pop-up toys.
- Safe plastic mirror—you can buy mirrors that allow the baby to see herself and the drivers.

Under-threes may enjoy:
- A few small stuffed animals, toy "people," or cars.
- Picture books (plastic bath books travel very well).
- Reuseable stickers that can be stuck onto the window.
- Magna Doodle-type toy, where you can draw pictures on a magnetic board with an attached drawing stick, without crayons or pens.

- Finger puppets.
- Masking tape! If you don't mind intentionally wasting it, children will have fun just sticking it, unsticking it, etc.
- Finger plays and singing with other family members.

Preschoolers may also like:
- Clipboard, paper, and markers.
- Books on tape (easily available at the public library).
- Car games and storytelling.

Mini LED flashlights are also great fun for toddlers and preschoolers if you are in the car at night (they are also excellent while hiking and at your campsite). They can be safely attached to a zipper or a strap to prevent children from putting them in the mouth.

Large zip-lock bags make handy containers for children's toys and books. They are waterproof, see-through, and lightweight. Children might enjoy writing their name on their bag ahead of time and decorating it.

If you bring things that are light and compact, toddlers and preschoolers can probably use most of them for their camp toys. When you reach the trailhead, place the zip-lock bag in the children's day packs. They can be responsible for carrying them on the hike to camp.

Simple car games

I Spy. One person says: "I spy, with my little eye, something that is yellow [choose a colour, shape, or other distinguishing feature]." The other person tries to guess what it is.

Song Grab-Bag. Spend some time with your children and write down the names of their (and your) favourite songs on separate pieces of paper. Mix them up in a small box or bag. While you are travelling,

take turns pulling one piece of paper out. Everyone in the car has to sing the song that's written on the paper.

I See One! Point out (and count) things like animals, types of cars, fences, barns, etc.

Fantasy Time. "If you could go anywhere in the world, where would you go and why?" "If you could be an animal or bird, what would you be and why?" Or, "If you found a bottle with a magic genie living in it, and you could have three wishes, what would they be and why?"

Continuous Story. One member of the family starts the story. The next person adds a line or two. And so on. Hilarious stories told by the whole family are the result. If your kids are not up for that, simply tell them a story. How about starting with: "One day a family went out for a hike. While they were hiking they saw … "

Story Bag. Ahead of time, write phrases on scraps of paper and place in a bag. When in the car, pull one out of the bag, and start a story.

Car sickness

Even small children can suffer from car sickness, and many adults (us among them) find car travel challenging because of motion sickness. Some tips:

- Keep a window open. Fresh air helps a lot.
- Make sure the temperature inside the car is not too hot.
- In vans, avoid seating children prone to car sickness in the rear seats.
- Avoid heavy meals before travelling.
- Keep a small bag of peppermints on hand. Having something in your stomach can help alleviate feelings of motion sickness, and peppermints are soothing on the digestive system. Sachiko travels with a permanent stash of mints in the glove compartment.
- Some people find the ginger in gingersnaps helpful.
- Kari and her son Rowan both wear acupressure bands around their wrists and find them very effective. They cost about five dollars and are available at drugstores. Even if you are already feeling motion sickness, put on the bands and they can alleviate the nausea.
- Be prepared in case someone *does* get sick. Have large zip-lock bags and a big box of wet wipes (or a bag of pre-moistened cloths) in your car.

Getting Ready is the Worst Part

"Have you packed the first-aid kit?"

"Where are your gloves, Elena?"

"No, Marin, you can't wear a dress and tights."

"The rainpants? Look in the bag on the hook in Elena's closet."

"Marin, you can't wear a dress and tights; we're going on a HIKE."

"How would I know where your gloves are, Elena? Didn't I buy you four pairs of gloves a few months ago? You can't find *any* of them?"

"Yes, you can wear your pink bandana, Marin. Yes, it looks very pretty."

"Do we have any snacks for the day pack?"

"The girls' water bottles? Aren't they in the library bag?"

"I know you're hot, Elena. Why don't you stand outside until we are ready?"

"Marin, you can wear a dress, but only if you wear leggings. Not tights. Don't ask ANYMORE."

"What time did we say we would pick them up?"

"Has anyone seen the camera? I thought I left it on the hall table."

"No, Elena, you can't sit in the car until Papa has taken the bike out and put the seats down."

"Has everyone gone pee?"

"Well, I think you should go again anyway."

"Why are you walking through the house with your dirty boots on?!"

"Okay, do we have everything?"

"I thought *you* locked the door."

"What? Now you want to go pee?"

"Aughh! I don't feel like going on a hike anymore!"

* * *

"But Mama, it'll be fun!"

INTRODUCTION TO DESTINATIONS

The destinations in this book are some of our favourite places in and around southern Vancouver Island and the Olympic Peninsula. Through the years of writing this book we have visited them over and over with our growing children, and each time we have experienced a new joy—found rare wildflowers on the trail, been lucky enough to sight whales, or simply enjoyed some relaxing family time. Though there are many other places to visit near Victoria, we keep going back to these, because they offer beauty, safety, and fun for each member of our families.

We have divided the destinations into three sections: day hikes, overnights, and long weekends. These are guidelines based on their distance from Victoria. Sometimes we spend more than one night at an overnight destination, and once we drove all the way to Carmanah for a day hike.

Below are some notes about the destinations, based on our experiences. You may find that walks we marked as easy are difficult for your family, or that the time it takes you to walk a trail is shorter than we have indicated. Just mark the difference in your book so you will remember for next time.

Driving times
- Driving times given are from downtown Victoria.
- All day trips are no more than an hour's driving time from Victoria.
- Overnights are no more than two hours' travelling time from Victoria.
- Long weekends are no more than four hours' travelling time from Victoria.

Our trail ratings
All trails are relatively easy hikes for adults. Our trail ratings are based on level of difficulty for young children. Most five- or six-year-olds could do any of the trails, but on "moderate" trails, toddlers will need help.

Easy. Mostly flat, usually wider than single file, with very little elevation gain. Suitable for toddlers to walk unassisted for the most part.

Moderate. Trail narrow, often single file only, with some steep sections, and other trail features (such as roots, rocks, mud). Elevation gain of up to 200 m. Toddlers will need assistance at times. Bring a child carrier or be prepared to carry your child as needed.

Challenging. We have listed only two of our destinations as challenging. The Lake Helen McKenzie trail is a moderate trail, but we have rated the hike challenging because of the distance—3.3 km one-way.

Toddlers could manage the trail, but it is a long way for a small person to walk. The Sombrio Point day trip from our Sombrio Beach destination is challenging because of the terrain; it is not suitable for a toddler because of drop-offs and often extremely muddy trail conditions. Families can hike the trail if toddlers are carried.

Time required

Times given are based on walking with our children aged two to six years. Of course, ability varies greatly and so will speed, so remember these are estimated times only. If you are carrying a baby in a child carrier, you will cover the distances much more quickly than if you are walking with small children in your group.

Campsites

- All camping is walk-in only tent camping.
- A portable camp stove is required (limited firepits at Ruckle Park and at Sidney Spit; fires may be banned at all destinations, subject to change without notice).

1

Becher Bay beach near Aylard Farm, East Sooke Park

Our rating: Moderate to challenging

Distance: 6 km (return)

Time: 3 – 4 hours (return)

Elevation change: No significant elevation change, but lots of ups and downs on the coast section

Biogeoclimatic zone/features: Coastal western hemlock: forest, ocean beach, intertidal zone, unused road

Land status: Capital Regional District (CRD) park

Best time to go: Any time. In winter the trail can be slippery. Be prepared, with sturdy shoes.

Fees: None

A day at East Sooke Park is enough to wash away the stress of life. On a sunny day the sea sparkles tropically, and the scent of the arbutus trees seems exotic. The coast trail dips down past enticing coves with sandy

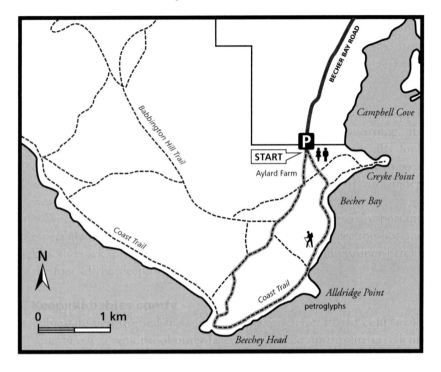

beaches, and rises along rock faces through arbutus, cedar, and Douglas-fir forests. Hikers walk over bare Metchosin volcanic rock that has not changed in over 50 million years, through ancient T'Sou-kes territory rich in trees, ferns, wildflowers, fungi, mushrooms, and lichens.

How to get there

Distance from Victoria: 35 km

Driving time: 1 hour

From Victoria take Highway 1 heading to Colwood and Sooke. Exit at the Colwood-Sooke turnoff onto Highway 14. Just past the 17 Mile House, turn left onto Gillespie Road. Follow Gillespie Road to the T-junction with East Sooke Road. Turn left and follow East Sooke Road to Becher Bay Road. Turn left onto Becher Bay, which leads into the parking lot at Aylard Farm. There are signs to East Sooke Park all the way from Gillespie Road, but some of them are hidden by overhanging branches.

Nearest facilities

Telephone: Sooke

Toilets: Outhouses at Aylard Farm parking lot
Hospital: Victoria General, 1 Hospital Way

About East Sooke Regional Park

Sooke is named for the T'Sou-kes people, who for thousands of years lived in and used the area now known as East Sooke Park. Their staple food was salmon, which they reef-netted around Becher Bay. They also harvested many types of shellfish, berries, and roots to augment their diet and store for winter months spent at Pedder Bay. The petroglyphs at Alldridge Point (a designated heritage site since 1927) and midden mounds bear witness to the T'Sou-kes.

In 1790, Spanish explorer Manuel Quimper was the first European to enter Sooke Inlet, but within five years, all lands north of Juan de Fuca Strait came under British control. A British sea captain named many places in the area (Becher Bay, Beechey Head, Alldridge Point) after his friends.

European settlers came to the Sooke area in the late 1800s. Iron and copper were mined for over 100 years at Iron Mine Bay and Mount Maguire, and much logging took place in the area now encompassed by the park. However, fishing was the most lucrative industry, and even today visitors will see fishing boats.

The Capital Regional District began purchasing land for the park in 1970. It is now the largest of the CRD parks.

Trail details

From the parking lot at Aylard Farm, follow the gravel path across the meadow towards the ocean. This meadow was once an apple orchard and pasture—all that remains of the original Aylard Farm. Pass the trail marker indicating Creyke Point and Coast Trail to your left, and continue to the stairs leading down to the beach. Here you can either head onto the beach for a picnic or follow the Coast Trail to your right towards Alldridge Point.

The Coast Trail winds through arbutus groves and up and down over rocks and roots. The ocean below sparkles in the sun as you pass by coves and climb promontories. Watch for small yellow markers bolted to the rock as the trail ascends a short, steep hill and flattens out by a wide rock overlooking a small beach. This is a great spot for a picnic, with easy access down to the water. Alldridge Point is two minutes farther along the trail (past a sign to Aylard Farm via the inland trail).

When you reach a sign for the trail to Beechey Head, you have reached Alldridge Point. Follow the yellow markers to the petroglyphs on the rocks.

Circle Route

From both Alldridge Point and Beechey Head a shorter inland route leads back to Aylard Farm and the parking lot.

From Alldridge Point, retrace your steps 10 metres to the sign indicating the inland trail to Aylard Farm. From Beechey Head, return to the Beechey Head trail sign and head along the trail leading away from the coast and into the forest. From both points the trails are steep, but soon join an old road, which is wide and easy to walk on, though occasionally steep. It is pleasant and cool through the forest all the way back to the parking lot at Aylard Farm. The inland trail from Beechey Head to Aylard Farm takes about 40 minutes. From Alldridge Point it is about a 20-minute walk.

A plaque indicates the largest petroglyph—a seal—but there are others to look for. Along the lower rocks you can search for more carvings, intertidal life, and small sea caves. This area is nearly impossible for toddlers to negotiate on their own; small children will have to be carried.

From the petroglyphs, retrace your steps to the signpost for Beechey Head and continue west along the Coast Trail, which becomes more challenging as it gets steeper and rockier. Toddlers will need to be carried when the trail ascends rock faces and follows cliff edges.

The trail rises up a steep rock face and follows the contours of the shoreline towards the next headland, passing through arbutus groves where in the summer, a warm, dry breeze cools hikers heated by the sun. Look for salal, kinnikinnick, Oregon grape, ferns, and other plants that have been growing here for millions of years.

Because much of the trail is on rock, it is difficult to follow in places. Keep an eye open for the yellow trail markers. Continue through the forest around coves and headlands. You are close to Beechey Head when the trail comes down a slight hill to a rock ledge about four feet high, which you will have to descend. Children will need help (so will some adults).

Shortly after this a sign indicates a forest trail to Aylard Farm. Continue on the Coast Trail for just a minute more until you reach a second sign for Beechey Head. Look for the yellow markers on a side trail through a chasm in the rocks and past a grove of lodgepole pines to Beechey Head itself: a large rock overlooking the ocean. You will have to scale the three-metre-high rock. Beware that on top there are no safety barriers, and it is a long fall down on all sides. Make sure children do not climb up unaccompanied by an adult.

What you might see

Once when we arrived on the beach at Aylard Farm, a seal was sunning itself on a rock not 5 m from where we stood. We watched it for a long time, then it slid in the water. We have never seen one so close since then, but we do often see them in the water. People luckier than us have seen whales and sea lions in Sooke Basin. Other creatures in East Sooke Park include deer, fox, wolves, squirrels, bald eagles, salamanders, frogs, and slugs. Cougars have also been sighted in the area. But the animals we most commonly come across are pet dogs.

What to bring
- Sturdy boots
- Child carrier
- Tree and flower identification guide
- Guide to mushrooms—the area is full of them!

Beach Treasure

"Pick this one up, Mummy," says three-year-old Rowan, pointing to a rock about the size of a small car. I laugh and tell him we can only pick up rocks smaller than his sand bucket. Together we find one I can manage, and I carefully turn it over. Underneath, a dozen tiny crabs scramble to get out of the way, and Rowan, wide-eyed, watches them in silence.

Rowan and I run across the smooth sand to a long, fallen tree trunk that reaches out across the beach to the water. From this spot we can see into tide pools teeming with life: anemones, limpets, chitons, pelagic goose barnacles on the rock wall, isopods, greenmark hermit crabs, rock weed, feather boa kelp.

After an hour or so of wandering along the beach, then picnicking, we decide to go for a walk along the Coast Trail. We climb up the stairs from the beach and start along the rocky path. Arbutus, Douglas firs, and cedars sway overhead. We think we see a yew tree; we know we see some huckleberries. We quietly pick our way over the roots and along the ragged trail for two or three minutes until suddenly Rowan stops, exclaims, and bends down. It's a calypso orchid growing right beside the path. We watch it for a few minutes then carry on, only to stop a second later to examine a chocolate fawn lily. We are not too worried about how far we get; there is just too much to see.

2

CENTENNIAL/HIGH RIDGE LOOP

FRANCIS/KING REGIONAL PARK

Skunk cabbage in the marsh

Our rating: Easy

Distance: 3 km (loop trail, return)

Time: 1 – 1.5 hours (return)

Elevation change: No significant elevation change, though trail does rise and fall throughout

Biogeoclimactic zone/features: Coastal Douglas-fir: forest, rocky outcropping, meadow

Land status: Capital Regional District (CRD) park

Best time to go: Any time. The first section of the trail through the bottomlands is very muddy in wet weather (or just after wet weather), and is criss-crossed by many large tree roots that are especially slippery when wet and may be challenging for toddlers. Our favourite time for this park is early spring—the skunk cabbage blooms are magnificent all through the marsh; the upper and lower forest canopies are coming alive with bright-green, new growth; and delicate white fawn lilies and purple shooting stars abound on the higher reaches of the trail.

Fees: None

This trail first follows bottomlands and skirts a marsh beneath the massive drooping branches of what feels like—and is—a primeval forest. The forests of Francis/King Park are more than 10,000 years old; the rocky hills on the High Ridge, millions of years old. As you leave the bottomlands and climb an easy grade to the ridge, the narrow trail takes you past luminous moss-covered trees and several huge hollowed-out tree stumps into pastoral Garry-oak meadows growing on rocky outcrops, with occasional glimpses of surrounding farmlands.

How to get there

Distance from Victoria: 13 km

Driving time: 20 minutes

Follow the Trans-Canada Highway in the direction of Duncan. Take the turnoff for Victoria General Hospital on Helmcken Road. At the first intersection, turn left onto West Burnside Road, then right onto

Centennial / High Ridge Trail Loop

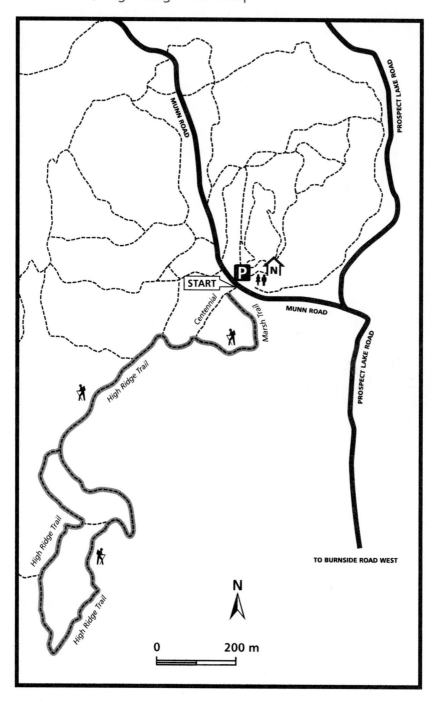

Prospect Lake Road. Watch for the sign for the park and take the left fork (Munn Road) where it branches off from Prospect Lake Road. Continue a few hundred metres along Munn Road. As you round the corner, you will see the Nature House on your right; turn in here and park in the gravel parking area.

Nearest facilities
Telephone: No public telephone, but there is a phone at the Nature House
Toilets: Outhouses located behind the Nature House
Hospital: Victoria General, 1 Hospital Way

About Francis/King Regional Park
The Coast Salish people found food and shelter in these forests and meadows, where they harvested camas bulbs, salal berries, horsetail sprouts, and medicinal plants. They also dried berries and made clothing and household objects from cedar.

What is now Francis/King Park is in fact two distinct parks. In the 1840s, James Francis purchased the land that is now the parkland east of Munn Road. He passed it on to his son, Thomas, who gave it to the province in 1960—this eastern parkland is Thomas Francis Park. The city of Victoria donated the land on the west side of Munn Road in 1967, and it was named for Freeman King (Freeman King Park). King was one of Victoria's earliest conservationists.

Trail details
From the parking lot directly in front of the Nature House, cross Munn Road. At the side of the road, pass through a split-rail-fence gate and walk straight down the first few metres of a short, steep slope. At the trail signpost, turn left (this is a side trail of the Centennial Trail that takes you alongside the marsh).

A packed-earth path starts under a Douglas fir, then continues through a stand of Garry oaks (and in summer under a long tunnel of leaves), until it passes underneath the sweeping branches of an ancient cedar, then descends to the bottomlands. You'll see the marsh on your left. In the early spring, the marsh is lit up with the bright, lemon-yellow blooms of skunk cabbage—they are elegant and dramatic, but "skunk" cabbage is no misnomer! They don't smell pretty. There are lots of exposed roots, and the path is often wet and muddy here.

The trail passes through a grove of silvery aspen trees, then comes to a trail marker indicating Centennial Trail to the left. Keep left and join the main Centennial Trail, which continues to straddle tangles of exposed roots, beside dark columns of towering trees, and stumps and branches dressed in lush, mossy garments and adorned with ferns. Shortly after you have crossed a small footbridge over a tiny creek, the trail starts a moderate climb up to the ridge.

Here bedrock is visible, as are open spaces and a changing canopy. The next trail marker indicates "High Ridge" to the left, and "Centennial" to the right. Take the High Ridge trail and climb to the ridge through a dense mixed forest of old-growth Douglas firs, cedars, and maples.

You will come to a trail marker indicating "High Ridge Trail" both to the left and to the right. You can go either way—the High Ridge trail is a 1-km loop that will bring you back to this point no matter which part of the loop you do first. If you keep right, you will climb a series of outcroppings to a high point where there is an open area (a good spot to sit and have a break). From there, the trail drops down, and after a short distance reclimbs the ridge. The final section of the trail along the ridge allows a few glimpses to the southeast over a wide valley of cleared farmland and a small lake, then skirts the perimeter of several private properties, including one where resident llamas may curiously gaze at you through a chain-link fence.

Just past the private homes, the trail begins to descend, eventually returning you to the beginning of the High Ridge loop. Rejoin the Centennial Trail and retrace your steps.

Nature House

What kind of tree was that? Why does skunk cabbage smell so bad? Why are some tree branches so curly? After your hike, stop in at the cozy little Nature House (open year-round). A naturalist can answer those intriguing questions, and there are fun hands-on displays for small children and lots of information about the recent history of the park. For current program information, see the CRD website (listed at the back of the book).

What you might see

Think small! The park is home to thousands of insects, spiders, and other creepy-crawlies. If you're lucky, you might hear and then see a Pacific Tree Frog; listen and look carefully in the swampy areas.

What to bring
• Tree and flower identification guide
• Binoculars—lots of woodpecker holes to zoom in on!

3 DAY TRIP
MT. NEWTON LOOP
JOHN DEAN PROVINCIAL PARK

Shaded, cool, and mossy Douglas-fir forest

Our rating: Moderate (some short steep sections, sometimes narrow)
Distance: 3 km (loop, return)
Time: 2.5 hours + (full loop)
Elevation change: No significant elevation change; steep ups and downs along sections of the trail
Biogeoclimatic zone/ features: Coastal Douglas-fir: forest, rocky, outcropping, meadow
Land status: Provincial park
Best time to go: Spring to fall. This loop can be a rewarding walk at any time of year. Spring is especially lovely, with magnificent displays of white fawn lilies, camas, and shooting stars.
Fees: None

John Dean Park is a lovely getaway—a wooded haven amongst the suburbs of East Saanich. It is hard to find, but once you are there, it feels like you are a million miles from a city. The towering old-growth Douglas firs soothe the soul, and the dark scent of damp earth makes breathing easy. Mosses and lichens give the forest an otherworldly feel. The trail is well sheltered, so walking in the park is pleasant and cool at any time of year.

How to get there
Distance from Victoria: 23 km
Driving time: 30 – 40 minutes

The road into John Dean Park is closed from November 1 to March 15. In winter, you can park at Carmanah Terrace and walk the 1 km up Dean Park road to the trailhead (around 30 minutes, uphill nearly all the way). The road is pleasant to walk along and is edged by a variety of trees and mosses that muffle sounds from development in the area.

However, the hike we describe may be too long for young children if you walk up first. You may wish to do a shorter loop instead (see map for suggested shorter loop).

From Victoria take the Patricia Bay Highway north to the airport turnoff at McTavish Road. Follow McTavish a short distance until it intersects with East Saanich Road, then turn left. Follow East Saanich Road past the Panorama Recreation Centre.

There is a provincial park sign on your right as you near Dean Park Road. Follow Dean Park Road 2.5 km through a housing development until you reach the park boundary; the last stretch of Dean Park Road takes you up the side of Mt. Newton to the parking lot.

Nearest facilities
Telephone: None in the park
Toilets: Outhouse at the trailhead
Hospital: Saanich Peninsula Hospital, 2166 Mt. Newton X Road

About John Dean Provincial Park
The Saanich people lived for thousands of years on the Saanich Peninsula before European settlement ("Saanich" is an anglicization of "shanets," which is believed to refer to "raising up"—either the profile of the Saanich peninsula visible from the ocean, or from the shape of Mt. Newton). The Saanich territory extended from one end of the peninsula to the other, and included many of the Gulf Islands and most of the San Juan Islands. From the sea, the Saanich harvested clams, oysters, mussels, and seaweed; fished for cod, halibut and salmon; and hunted seals and porpoises. Bulrushes from marshes were woven into multi-purpose mats, cedar bark was used to make rope and baskets, and willow bark was made into fine twine for nets and fishing lines.

Lauwelnew (Mt. Newton) provided refuge to the Saanich people during post-glacial floods. It is said that Saanich ancestors used a giant cedar rope to secure their canoe on Lauwelnew ("place of escape") until flood waters receded, and that remnants of the rope can still be seen by those

Mt. Newton Loop

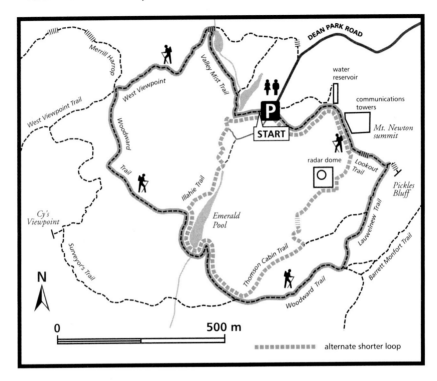

who know where to look. The Tsawout people of the Saanich Nation believe that the "Thunder Being" lives in a cave on Lauwelnew—their sacred place—and that he is the communicator between this world and the sky world.

Following European contact, smallpox, measles, and tuberculosis decimated much of the First Nations population. In 1852 the Saanich signed the Douglas treaties, and European settlement of the lands followed soon after.

In 1921, Saanich resident John Dean donated the first 32 hectares of the park, with other residents donating additional lands over the years. Remnants of their homesteads can be seen in the park.

Trail Details

This hike is a loop made with five interconnecting trails. The first part of the hike—the short Valley Mist trail—is not clearly indicated on the large trail map posted at the John Dean parking lot (it is shown, but is not named).

From the trailhead next to the map, take the path marked "Valley

Mist"—a one-metre wide, well-graded, packed-earth trail lined with stones, which leads down a moderately steep slope into an old-growth Douglas-fir forest that is shaded, cool and mossy at all times of year. Abundant salal, Oregon grape, and swordferns carpet the understory of the forest.

After 150 m, you will reach the first junction. Keep right on the Valley Mist trail, and along this flat stretch look for decaying nurse logs supporting young saplings, as well as fungi, moss, and lichens. The trail skirts a large lily pond on the right—home to Pacific Tree Frogs and Pacific Coast Newts, both of which can be seen by patient and still onlookers in spring.

At the far end of the pond, a trail junction marks the end of the short Valley Mist trail and the beginning of the West Viewpoint trail (the right-hand trail is unmarked). Take the wooden staircase to the left, and then begin a steady climb through the forest for about 150 m until the trail levels off, then narrows to single-file, continuing to rise gently into a drier ecosystem characterized by a less dense canopy and the presence of arbutus trees.

After a short distance, you will reach a third trail junction. On the left is the beginning of the Woodward trail (straight ahead is the final stretch of the West Viewpoint trail; on the right is the Merrill Harrop trail).

Follow the Woodward trail down a hill; the path is somewhat rocky, criss-crossed by roots, and bordered by overgrown salal bushes. There is a stagnant pool on the left. The trail winds through a dark forest of cedars and Douglas fir and past several more dark pools and stone "bridges," where the ground is swampy. The forest floor is littered with huge deadfall, mostly covered with brilliant green mosses.

After about 20 minutes, you will come to a junction. On the left is the Illahie trail (a convenient way to shorten this hike—a 5-minute walk will bring you right back to the parking lot, taking you past the

Thomson Cabin shortcut

The Thomson Cabin trail provides another shortcut back to the parking lot—the trail rises through beautiful Garry-oak meadows that are covered in shooting stars in the spring, down a steep hill to the Thomson Cabin site, then up a flight of stairs and uphill until you come out at a gravel road and the first of two federal-government radar towers. Follow the gravel road to the right for 10 minutes back to the parking lot.

Enjoying the trail at John Dean Park

site of John Dean's cabin and an old water pump).

Carry on to the right (still on the Woodward trail). The path is mostly level, but full of tree roots and rocks. You'll soon reach the end of another stagnant pond and see the signpost indicating "John Dean's Emerald Pool"—a name which seems to take considerable poetic licence, as the water is murky and dark. A stone bridge crosses Canyon Creek at the end of the pool, and with an initial switchback, the trail begins a steady climb into more open forest. Look for beautiful displays of white fawn lilies in early spring.

Just beyond a massive shelf of split rock that looks like giant-sized blocks in an ancient stone wall, two side trails branch off from the Woodward trail: to the left—the Thomson Cabin trail; to the right—the Surveyor's trail.

Continue straight ahead on the Woodward trail. This is a particularly beautiful stretch, as you walk through more open forest and along sunny rock outcroppings graced with pretty meadows (bright with wildflowers in spring)—an ideal spot for a picnic. Tread very lightly if you sit down off-trail; the ecosystem is delicate and very sensitive.

Once past the ridge, look for the signpost where the Lauwelnew trail meets the Woodward trail (this is the end of the Woodward trail; straight on is the beginning of the Barrett Montfort trail). Follow the Lauwelnew trail to the left, up a steep hill past rock outcroppings, Garry oaks and arbutus.

Keep right at an unmarked fork (there is no trail signpost; to the left is the short Fern Dell trail, which joins up with the Thomson Cabin trail). Stay on the Lauwelnew trail, which continues to climb until it ends at the Lookout trail.

Expecting the lookout to be at the summit of Mt. Newton, we were quite surprised the first time we came here when we saw that the trail pitched steeply *downhill*. In fact, it drops quickly, down four sets of well-built stairs, ending at a three-metre-wide rocky outcropping with a precipitous drop-off (Pickles Bluff). The viewpoint affords a spectacular view, but there are no barriers and some parents may be too nervous to enjoy the panorama. Children need a parent's firm hand. This might not be a good choice for children who like complete liberty of movement.

There is a sweeping 180-degree view to the southeast, taking in Sidney, Sidney Island, the San Juan Islands, Saanich farmlands, Mt. Baker, Bear Hill, Observatory Hill, Mt. Douglas, and even the distant downtown Victoria skyline.

To end this hike, first climb back up the 75 wooden steps, and then, just beyond, up another 63 rock steps (Sachiko's toddler enjoyed these immensely). You'll come out at a gravel road, which leads to the Coast Guard Radar Site on the actual summit of Mt. Newton. This site is a brutal departure from the beauty of the trails, as treetops have been lopped off, presumably to assist with the radar signals.

Turn left onto the first gravel road, then right onto the wider Ministry of Transportation road, which leads downhill about 300 m, directly back to the parking lot.

What you might see
- Black-tailed deer
- Pacific Coast Newts
- Pileated woodpeckers
- Pacific Tree Frogs
- Fawn lilies and shooting stars

What to bring
- Sweater or light coat. Even in summer, John Dean Park is shady and cool. In spring and fall, we always bring gloves and a warm hat.
- Tree and flower identification guides.
- Guide to mushrooms—the area is full of them!
- Binoculars—it's fun to identify landmarks from Pickles Bluff.

4

DAY TRIP
PROSPECTORS' TRAIL
GOLDSTREAM PROVINCIAL PARK

Forest shapes and textures around every corner

Our rating: Moderate

Distance: 2 – 3.6 km (return)

Time: 2 – 3 hours (return)

Elevation change: No significant elevation change. Trail narrow in many areas, some steep sections. Toddlers will need help.

Biogeoclimatic zone/features: Coastal Douglas-fir: forest

Land status: Provincial park

Best time to go: Any time. Most of the hike is in the shade, so this would be a nice choice on a hot day. In light rain, the forest canopy keeps you from getting too wet. If you don't like crowds, avoid salmon-spawning season (late October to December), when the parking lot is usually packed to capacity.

Fees: Day-use parking fee. Bring cash. See the BC Parks website for current rates (website url at the back of this book).

This is a magical hike under gigantic 600-year-old Douglas fir and western redcedar draped in mossy robes, past impressive slabs of rock and boulders, over a few boardwalk footbridges, and up to a sunny lookout on a green-carpeted outcrop in an arbutus grove. The trail is fairly steep at first, then slowly winds and climbs up the slope of a ridge above Goldstream River. At the high point, it has views to forested hills to the south, on the other side of the highway. Less frequented than the other popular trails in the park, this hike provides all kinds of forest shapes, textures, sights, and sounds, around every corner.

Prospectors' Trail

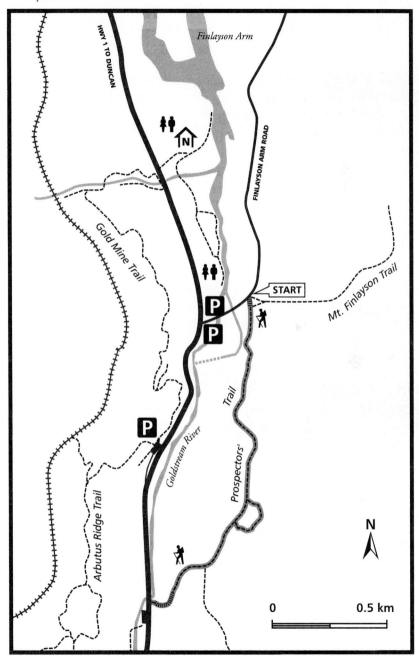

How to get there
Distance from Victoria: 16 km
Driving time: 30 minutes
Bus Access: #58 Langford Meadows. Get off at Sooke Lake Road. You must walk through the provincial park campground to reach the trail, which will add extra time to your hike.

If driving, take the Trans-Canada (Highway 1) north in the direction of Duncan. Just past Langford Lake, the highway crosses the Goldstream Provincial Park boundary, with the park bordering the highway on both sides. The main parking area for trails and the Nature House is near the junction of the highway and Finlayson Arm Road; look for the sign on the right just before the turnoff. If there is space, park in the small gravel parking area immediately to your right.

Note: You may notice on park maps that it is possible to access the Prospectors' Trail from the south end (from a small parking lot off the highway, south of the day-use area).

We don't advise this, because the trailhead is on the opposite side of the highway from the parking area, and you have only two ways to reach it: run across the highway (dangerous, and that's if you ever get a break in the traffic), or try to go under the highway beneath the bridge (only possible if the river is low enough). Also, there are no outhouses at the trailhead, or anywhere on the Prospectors' Trail.

Nearest facilities
Telephone: Freeman King Visitor Centre, a 15-minute walk past the day-use parking lot along the Goldstream River
Toilets: Outhouses at the main day-use parking lot; indoor bathrooms at the Visitor Centre
Hospital: Victoria General, 1 Hospital Way

About Goldstream Provincial Park
Like much of Vancouver Island, this is another area rich in First Nations history. The Goldstream estuary was treasured by the Malahat and Wsanec. Families came together in a fall village at Goldstream, where they harvested chum salmon, clams, and crabs, and built smokehouses along the water to prepare foods for winter. They also planted potatoes and cultivated fruit trees near the present-day Nature House.

With European settlement came treaties (1850) and establishment of reserves (1913). A Royal Engineer discovered gold in the creek and set off a small gold rush in the 1860s, hence the name "Goldstream."

Old mining shafts and tunnels remain. The Greater Victoria Water Board made the area into parkland in 1958.

Trail details

From the day-use parking area, walk across the bridge and down Finlayson Arm Road a few hundred metres. You will see a trail marker on the right with safety information for the Mt. Finlayson access and a park map. This is the trailhead for the Mt. Finlayson trail as well as for the Prospectors' Trail.

If you like stairs (and lots of 'em!), head straight up the steep concrete staircases to the Prospectors' Trail. An alternate beginning is to follow the gentle grade of the first part of the Mt. Finlayson trail for less than five minutes; you will soon come to a fork. The right fork reconnects in a matter of minutes with the Prospectors' Trail—and you miss the stairs.

Viewpoint at site of prospectors' holes

You will be walking along a dirt trail under the cover of towering old-growth Douglas fir and western redcedar in a temperate rainforest. It is a long, long way up to patches of sky! Listen for the ancient trees creaking in the wind. At the first junction, about 250 m past the top of the stairs, keep to the right and continue along the ridge for about 1 km. For the most part, the trail is narrow, although it widens through flatter sections. It ascends gradually, with some moderately steep sections that have root or lumber "stair" supports.

Once you have moved from the darker forest onto higher ground and crossed the second of two boardwalk bridges, you will come to a trail junction. There is a trail sign here, but at our last visit, the trail information was not posted. This side trail leads to a nice viewpoint, the site of prospectors' holes for copper.

Take the side trail and head up the winding path. As you near the high point, you'll see large rock outcroppings covered in luminous green mosses, and the reddish trunks and peeling bark of arbutus trees. At the top you can sit comfortably on a rocky bench and gaze off into the distance, or lie down for a nap in the sun.

Continuing past the viewpoint, you will come back down again to reconnect with the main Prospectors' Trail. Turn right to hike back out to the trailhead. Plan on more than two hours for the whole trip.

If you wish to extend your hike, the final .5 km to where the trail meets the highway is also a lovely walk, with ups and downs. The scenery is similar to that on the first part of the trail, but different enough to warrant a look. When you reach the 53 stairs heading down, turn around and head back; otherwise you will come out at the busy highway. With the extra distance, expect to spend about three hours for the whole trip.

Visitor Centre

If you get back to the parking lot but aren't ready to go home yet, the 15-minute walk to the Freeman King Visitor Centre is pleasant and easy, following a wide, level path alongside Goldstream River to the estuary. Start at the northern end of the parking area. The nature centre has hands-on displays and a bookstore, as well as interpreters who can answer your questions. Before your hike, you can call ahead (250-478-9414) for current program information.

What you might see

The principal interest on this trail is the incredible understory and canopy of the forest. During salmon-spawning season, you will see the chum salmon in the river just before you access the trail. In December and January, look for bald eagles, who come to feed on the salmon carcasses in the estuary. The best viewing area is near the Nature Centre.

What to bring

This is a good place for children to bring a magnifying glass to examine forest treasures—there are all kinds of interesting bark textures, tiny plants, and more, to see up-close. Try paper and pencil for texture rubbings.

Forest Bouquet

There are autumn-hued leaves all over the path.

"Look, Mama!"

She has collected her favourite, perfectly shaped ovals, each of which narrows at one end into a fine, serrated point. She grasps their firm stems in her small hand. There are reds, golds, and earthy browns, and they are spread out like a small fan.

"Look, Mama, it's a bouquet!"

5

DAY TRIP
SANDCUT BEACH
WESTERN FOREST PRODUCTS RECREATION AREA

Sandcut Beach, looking to the southwest

Our rating: Moderate

Distance: 200 m to the beach (one-way)

Time: 15 minutes (one-way). Note: You can walk from Sandcut a further 1.5 km along the cobble beach to Desolation Creek and towards Jordan River (all one-way). Count on 1.5 hours (return) for Desolation Creek and 3.5 hours (return) to Jordan River.

Elevation change: No significant elevation loss, but access to beach is moderately steep

Biogeoclimatic zone/features: Coastal western hemlock: forest, ocean beach

Land status: Western Forest Products recreational area

Best time to go: Any time. Because this is a lesser-known destination, we prefer to come here than to the more popular French and China beaches. In the winter, when the weather is moody, we can have the beach all to ourselves. However, in wet weather the trail to the beach can get muddy and slippery and will be difficult for small children, and for adults carrying children in child carriers.

Fees: None

Point No Point visible in the distance

and steeply through second-growth forest, with the occasional old-growth giant towering above the ferns, salal, and younger trees.

The trail levels off at the bottom of the slope; here sections of boardwalk and three low, rail-less bridges cross shallow McManus Creek (use caution when crossing, as the trail is maintained by Western Forest Products and is not up to the same standard as most BC Parks trails).

Once over the creek, you will climb a short hill and come down again on the other side. Open sky beyond signals the edge of the forest and arrival at the beach.

ALONG SANDCUT BEACH
TO DESOLATION CREEK
AND JORDAN RIVER

Our rating: Easy

Distance: 1.5 km to Desolation Creek; 3 km to Jordan River (all return)

Time: 1.5 hours to Desolation Creek; 3.5 hours to Jordan River (all return)

Elevation change: None

Sandcut's cobble beach stretches east and west as you leave the trail under a natural gate formed by an uprooted tree lying on its side. To the south, across Juan de Fuca Strait, are the magnificent snow-capped peaks of Washington's Olympic Mountains. To the east you can see the silhouette of Point No Point (so-called because the point of land can only be seen from certain angles).

Head west (to your right). The cobble beach is great fun for children, with beautiful stones and all kinds of beach treasures that will have little ones walking at a snail's pace! At low tide, there are some stretches of level, firm sand that make for faster walking.

Just beyond a point of land at the western end of the beach is Desolation Creek and an unobstructed view towards Jordan River.

The walk to Desolation Creek is a perfect distance for toddlers. If Desolation Creek is low enough to ford or hop across, parents carrying children in a backpack, and older children, might like to continue the walk all the way to Jordan River. Check tide tables to make sure you will be able to get back again.

START AT JORDAN RIVER

It is also possible to do this walk in the opposite direction. To begin at Jordan River, park at the Western Forest Products gravel parking area, where there is a tri-panel display about the company and its practices (on your left, as you enter the community of Jordan River—not the parking lot next to the bridge over Jordan River).

Get out on the beach and turn left, walking east in the direction of Point No Point. Keep in mind that if Desolation Creek is high, you will not be able to walk all the way to Sandcut Beach.

What you might see
- Mink (sometimes you can see them hunting for intertidal fish, waterfowl, or small mammals)
- Velella (type of jellyfish)
- Cormorants
- Purple or green shore crabs

What to bring
Even if it's a sunny day, don't leave home without your raingear. The weather can be completely different here than in Victoria. Rubber boots are fine for the short trail to the beach and are fun for splashing in the water. Binoculars will make it easier for you to see creatures in the water, or to get close-ups of passing boats. You might even see a whale. At Jordan River, you can watch surfers do their moves.

6

Witty's Beach on a sunny afternoon

Our rating: Easy

Distance: 1.2 km (one-way)

Time: 20 minutes (each way) and time to explore the beach and spit

Elevation change: No significant elevation change, but a moderately steep descent for the first 300 m

Biogeoclimatic zone/features: Coastal western hemlock: forest, salt marsh, spit, ocean beach

Land status: Capital Regional District (CRD) park

Best time to go: Any time. This hike is enjoyable in all seasons. With rubber boots and good raingear, the flat stretches of beach and mud flats at low tide are great fun, even during winter rains. In early spring, the trail is graced with beautiful spring wildflowers, including white fawn lily and indigo camas. In the summer, this beach is popular, so expect to share it and the trail with lots of people. We try to avoid weekends and come during the week, if we can.

Fees: None

Witty's Lagoon has been formed where a coastal bay (Parry Bay) is bordered by a protective sand spit. The beach trail starts in a woodland of Douglas fir, bigleaf maple and western redcedar, then passes through a complex array of ecosystems with features including a creek, a beautiful waterfall, a salt marsh, the expansive lagoon, and grasslands, coming out at a wide, flat, sandy beach with clear views past Race Rocks across Juan de Fuca Strait to Washington's Olympic Mountains.

How to get there
Distance from Victoria: 18 km
Driving time: 25 minutes
Follow the Trans-Canada Highway (Highway 1) in the direction of Duncan. Take the Colwood exit and follow Sooke Road through Colwood past Royal Roads University, then get into the left-hand-turn lane. Turn left onto Metchosin Road. Follow Metchosin Road past the gravel pits and past the "Welcome to Metchosin" sign a little further on. You will see a sign for Witty's Lagoon Regional Park near the Tower Road entrance. Carry on—the main park entrance is a few kilometres further, and well marked with another sign. Turn off to your left, just opposite a golf course. Park in the gravel parking lot.
Bus: #54 Metchosin or #55 Happy Valley. Contact Busline at 250-382-6161 for schedules.

Nearest facilities
Telephone: No public telephone, but there is a phone at the Nature Centre (open seasonally).
Toilets: Outhouses located at the trailhead just past the Nature Centre, and also at the beach.
Hospital: Victoria General, 1 Hospital Way.

About Witty's Lagoon
Witty's Lagoon was home to the Ka-Kyaaken, a Coastal Salish people. From the abundant sea, the Ka-Kyaaken reef-netted salmon and harvested sea urchins, sea cucumbers, mussels, barnacles, snails, whelks, and chiton. They gathered camas bulbs and used rich forest resources to make baskets, canoes, and clothing. Within the park boundaries are five shell middens (an archeological term meaning "garbage heap"), two of which were at fortified locations that had surrounding trenches and wooden palisades.

The Klallam people (a Coast Salish First Nation originating in the Olympic Peninsula) came to the area in the 19th century and mixed with First Nations in the area known today as Becher Bay. Race Rocks (visible from Witty's Beach) was known as "xwayen"—fast-flowing water—in the Klallam language.

In 1850, James Douglas (of the Hudson's Bay Company) negotiated treaties with nine Salish First Nations in Victoria, Metchosin and Sooke. He purchased all the land from Pedder Bay to Albert Head for £43 worth of blankets. First Nations were promised rights to hunt on unsettled lands and to carry on fisheries "as formerly".

In 1851, the Witty's Lagoon area was purchased by European settlers and farmed. In 1867, the Witty family bought the land. The Ka-Kyaakan band continued to live there until the late 1850s, then moved to Becher Bay. They continued to use the lagoon until 1878. In 1966 the CRD purchased land from the Witty family and has managed the area since 1969.

Trail details

A two-metre-wide packed-gravel path starts at the far end of the parking lot, next to the small nature house, then descends a moderately steep slope a few hundred metres to a trail junction. The left-hand trail (Lagoon Trail) skirts the lagoon on its northern side and is a very enjoyable hike on its own. Carry on straight ahead over the wooden footbridge and across Bilston Creek, which flows around lush mossy boulders under a canopy of gnarled bigleaf maples.

The footbridge leads to a well-fenced lookout over the beautiful Sitting Lady Falls, where Bilston Creek tumbles 50 m over volcanic pillow rock (look for the unique pillow shapes) and down to the saltwater lagoon.

Bilston Creek tumbles over volcanic rock, then drops 50 m to the lagoon

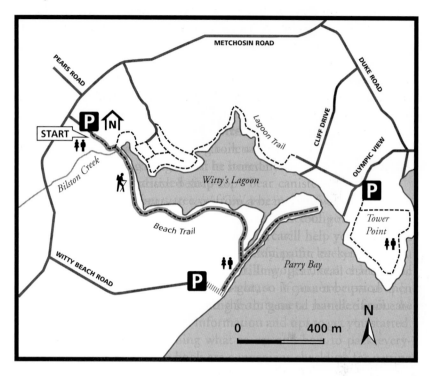

The waterfall marks the boundary between the freshwater zone and the saltwater zone at high tide.

From the viewpoint, the trail narrows to about a metre wide, with wooden handrails to help negotiate the initial drop in elevation along the steepest sections of the trail, from high above the lagoon down to the bottomlands. This part of the trail travels through a rich Douglas-fir forest, the path bordered by a sea of huge swordferns with the occasional arbutus, western redcedar, or bigleaf maple (beautiful in spring, with fragrant yellow-green catkins dangling from the branches).

The trail gradually becomes less steep, and the forest opens up as you near sea level. Enormous blackberry brambles cover an entire hillside to the right, marking the area of the old farmstead.

A low wooden footbridge crosses over a swampy salt marsh and a trickle of creek. Just beyond the footbridge, there is a fork in the trail. Keep right (the left-hand trail is an unauthorized trail bordering the lagoon edge, which has had heavy use and is causing damage). Once over a small hill, the trail leaves the forest completely, begins to cross the flood plain, and passes grassland, several magnificent Garry oaks, and a large stand of cottonwood trees, just before arriving at the beach

A gnarly arbutus on the trail near the beach

barrier spit that divides the ocean from the salt marsh.

This is the end of the trail. Outhouses are to the right, near an established picnic area. The 300-metre long sand spit is bordered by piles of driftwood—large, sculptural bleached logs thrown up onto the sand by waves and storms.

We like to walk to the end of the sand spit (near the homes on Tower Point), then explore the salt marsh. This is an excellent place to watch birds and on a hot day there is plenty of soft sand and warm, shallow water for playing in.

What you might see

We have frequently seen great blue herons standing elegantly against the horizon on the mud flats. Look also for herring gulls, mallard ducks, cormorants, kingfishers, jays, and even loons (over 160 species of birds

Bird Trill

Rowan and I are walking along together. The trail is beautiful, but we are grumpy and not enjoying each other's company. Rowan would have preferred to stay home and is stopping and stalling every few steps. I need to reach the beach, to find a place where we can sit down in comfort and listen to the lap of the waves. We grumble and groan along until, just as we approach the beach, a bird trills from a tree near the shore.

"Ah, a beach welcome," says Rowan. He turns and gives me a big smile. Our grumpiness is gone in an instant, and we are together experiencing a magical moment.

How did they do that?

The first time we came to Witty's Lagoon in the summer, we arrived out of breath at the beach. We'd forgotten our child carrier and had carried our toddler almost all the way. When we looked around us, we saw families toting big coolers, beach umbrellas, and all kinds of bulky gear. We couldn't imagine how they'd hauled all that stuff down the trail. That's when we found out that there is a direct beach access, with no hike involved, outside the park boundary.

Just beyond the outhouse near the beach is a long flight of wooden steps. For those who just want the beach, but don't want the hike, it is possible to drive to a parking lot above the stairs, and then unload.

To reach this access, instead of turning in at the Witty's Lagoon parking lot, carry on along Metchosin Road 500 m and look for "Witty Beach Road" on your left. This narrow country lane takes you to a parking lot, which in summer is frequently overflowing, with cars parked up and down the roadside, as well as in the lot. It's a five-minute walk down the stairs to the beach.

have been documented here), as well as harbour seals and sea lions in the strait. On the beach, you may find brown bull kelp, bleached coraline red algae (branch-like), clam, mussel, scallop and limpet shells, acorn barnacles, hermit crabs, red rock crabs, and purple sea stars.

What to bring

- Binoculars. You can look up close at the Haystock Islands, and at Race Rocks further out (the most southern point of Canada's west coast), zoom in on freighters in the strait, and watch birds on the lagoon and mud flats.
- Windbreakers. It may seem warm up at the parking lot, but when it gets windy at the water, it can be really cold.
- Rubber boots and a change of pants or raingear. What's water for if you can't play in it? Bathing suit or quick-dry shorts and sunscreen are also must-haves in good weather.
- Beach toys. Something to dig with, something to collect things in.
- Kite. Strong winds and wide stretches of mud flats make this an ideal place for kite flying.

7

OVERNIGHT
MYSTIC BEACH
JUAN DE FUCA PROVINCIAL PARK

Waterfall at Mystic Beach

Our rating: Moderate (with a challenging section at the very end)
Distance: 2 km (one-way)
Time: 1 – 1.5 hours (one-way)
Elevation loss: 100 m
Biogeoclimatic zone/features: Coastal western hemlock: forest, ocean beach, intertidal zone
Land status: Provincial park
Best time to go: Summer. Avoid this trail in wet weather; extremely muddy is an understatement. The beach is exposed to winds and offers little shelter from nasty weather—enjoy it in the sun. Those seeking quiet should avoid weekends, as easy access makes this a popular overnight destination, and Mystic is the first (or last) site on the multi-day Juan de Fuca Trail hike, which makes for lots of traffic.
Fees: Day-use parking fee. If you are camping, parking is included in self-registration camping fee. Bring cash; no other payment options. For current fee information, visit the BC Parks website (listed at the back of the book).

Mystic Beach

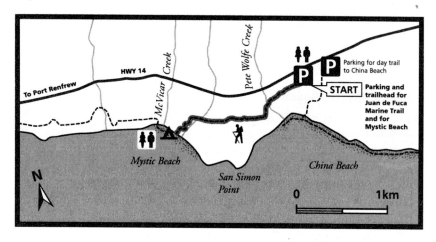

A rooty trail winds through a cool, sun-dappled second-growth forest, with several sections of boardwalk, plank bridges, and a suspension bridge high above Pete Wolfe Creek. The gradual descent to the ocean ends with a final scramble down to a gently curving crescent of cobble and fine, flat sand, backed by high cliffs and graced by a cascading waterfall. The soft sand is perfect for toddlers, while shallow cave hollows under the sculpted sandstone cliffs offer hours of exploring for older children.

How to get there
Distance from Victoria: 65 km
Driving time: 1.5 hours

From Victoria, take Highway 1 heading north towards Duncan. Exit at the Langford overpass to connect with the Veterans Memorial Parkway through Langford, which intersects with Highway 14 to Sooke. Turn right in the direction of Sooke.

About 35 km west of Sooke, you'll pass the turnoff for the China Beach Provincial Park campground. Keep going another kilometre and take the next turnoff to the China Beach day-use area and the Juan de Fuca East Trailhead (also the trailhead to Mystic Beach). There are two parking areas; to be closest to the trailhead, park in the first gravel parking area on the right.

Nearest facilities
Telephone: Jordan River
Gas: Sooke

Day trips

We usually don't do day hikes from Mystic, as the only further hiking is to carry on along the Juan de Fuca Trail towards Bear Beach. Bear Beach is 7 km from Mystic, and the first part of the trail is mostly through dense shrub and forest, with no views.

Bad-weather planning

Come prepared for very wet weather. Good raingear for everyone in the family, an efficient rain fly for your tent, and a tarp to set up for a cooking area will give you the shelter you need to make the best of it! Mystic's dreamy landscape can be at its best in fog and misting rain. Being tent- or tarp-bound in inclement weather is an opportunity to use your imagination, sit around and tell stories, play card games, sing—all the things you never do at home because you are too busy. The trail can be very slippery when wet, and seriously muddy as well. Wear good hiking shoes, ankle-height if possible, with suitable grip.

What you might see

Seals, sea lions, whales, eagles, otters, mink.

What to bring

- Good walking shoes that can withstand serious mud.
- An extra pair of shoes to use at the beach. Old tennis shoes, aqua socks, or rubber boots make exploring in the water less uncomfortable.
- A tarp with ropes to spread over a section of the campsite so you will have some protection if the weather turns ugly.
- Binoculars for seeking out whales.

Hidden Treasure

"Look, pirates have been here," says Rowan. I turn to follow him under the cascading waterfall into the cave behind. We squeal with delight as the spray catches me. Rowan marches to the back of the cave and points. There in the corner is a stack of stones, carefully tucked away far from curious eyes. "Hidden treasure, do you think?" he asks.

As he digs, I wander around the little cave. In each crevice and on every shelf I find a small stack of stones or shelves—someone's art, left behind for others to admire. I have found my treasure.

8

OVERNIGHT
RUCKLE PROVINCIAL PARK
SALTSPRING ISLAND

Tent sites in rocky meadows looking over Swanson Channel

Our rating: Easy

Distance: 500 m – 1 km (one-way)

Time: 5 – 20 minutes (one-way)

Elevation change: None

Biogeoclimatic zone/features:
Coastal Douglas-fir: forest, meadow,
ocean beach, intertidal zone

Land status: Provincial park

Best time to go: May to October (the park is open year-round, but there are no park services from October to mid-April)

Fees: Day-use parking fee. If camping overnight, parking included in camping fee. Bring cash. For current fee information, visit the BC Parks website (listed at the back of the book).

We nearly always make this our first camping destination of the year in early May, because the easy accessibility makes it the perfect place to do a test run. What is lovely about this park is the mix of field, forest, and coastal scenery. Situated on a peaceful corner of Saltspring Island,

Ruckle Park

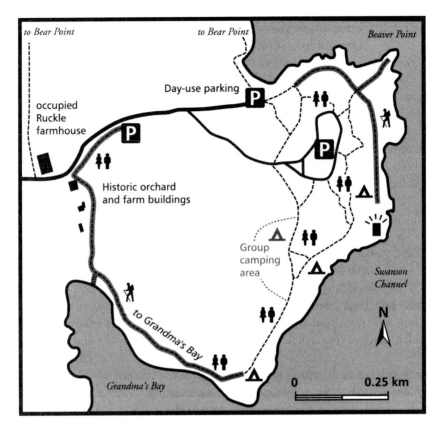

Ruckle offers beautiful tent sites on grassy bluffs overlooking Swanson Channel, with easy short and long walks to a sheltered bay, the old Ruckle farm, along gentle grades in the woodlands, and above the rocky coastline. There are also scrambles along driftwood, rock shelves and small gravelly beaches rich with tidal life.

How to get there

Distance from Victoria: 20 km to Swartz Bay ferry terminal; once on Saltspring, 10 km to park gate.

Driving time: Allow 30 minutes driving to Swartz Bay plus 35-minute passenger ferry ride, then a 10-minute drive to Ruckle Park.

From Victoria, drive 25 km to the Swartz Bay ferry terminal. Line up for the Saltspring Island ferry to Fulford Harbour. As you leave the ferry, you will drive past a number of quirky shops and then up a short slope to a T-junction. Turn right (left will take you into Ganges) and follow Beaver Point Road for 10 km. The road becomes a dead end and takes you right into the park. You will pass a parking area for the group camping site. Park in any lot past the service road—closest to the service road is better for access to the more secluded sites.

Note: A parking fee applies to day-users only. If you are camping overnight, you do not have to pay this fee.

Nearest facilities

Telephone: Heritage farm parking lot (as you drive into the park, on your right past the last farm building)
Groceries and supplies: Fulford Harbour, Patterson's grocery store
Showers: Fulford Harbour Marina
Laundromat: Several in Ganges, two at the marinas
Hospital: Ganges: Lady Minto Hospital, 135 Crofton Road
Park services available: None. With the changes in BC Parks services, there is only a "camp host" who oversees the campground. The host is set up in a camper or trailer at one of the sites closest to the parking area.

About Ruckle Provincial Park

Saltspring Island was a seasonal home for Coast Salish First Nations for thousands of years, and there were once large permanent settlements on the island as well. Both the Wsanec people (Saanich Peninsula) and the Cowichan travelled to the island to harvest abundant natural resources. The earliest herring runs were at Fulford Harbour. Cedar boughs were placed near the shore so herring would lay roe on them, and the herring was dried into a delicacy and stored for winter.

Located at Beaver Point on Saltspring Island, Ruckle Park is named for the family of Henry Ruckle. An immigrant from Ireland, he came to Saltspring in 1872. He and his family homesteaded the land that is now part of the park. In 1974, the family donated most of their property for the provincial park, but they still raise sheep on a small parcel of land, making the farm one of the oldest continuously run family farms in British Columbia.

Trail details

PARKING LOT TO TENT SITES

At the second parking lot after the service road, there is a sign indicating "Walk-in Camping." This trail heads left 500 m through forest directly to the lighthouse and the very closest tent sites (a five- to ten-minute walk). The second trail to the right leads past the group-camp-

ing area, and takes you through forest towards the sites farthest from the parking lot (up to 20 minutes, depending on the site you choose). Both trails are wide, level, and easy, although they are sometimes quite muddy if it has been wet.

TENTING AREA

In an area starting from near the lighthouse and extending south, there are 74 walk-in tent sites. Most sites are on grassy meadows on the bluffs above the water, but a few are nestled in trees to the right of the gravel path that runs through the tenting area.

Tide pool treasure at Grandma's Bay

The most secluded sites are those farthest from the lighthouse, to the south. To reach these, go past the group-camping area, and continue along the gravel path. The sites numbered 64 to 74 are on a rocky outcrop among arbutus and other evergreens, but still have lovely water views. They are also very windy sites; in stormy weather consider nearby sites in the shelter of trees.

Day trips

EXPLORING TIDE POOLS

The rock shelves below the tenting meadow are home to fascinating pools of intertidal life (look for limpets, anemones, sea stars, oysters, crabs, and mussels). Bring shoes with good non-slip soles (water slippers are perfect). Access involves some climbing. Children need an adult along for safety; there is wave danger at times from the wake of large vessels. Grandma's Bay (near Ruckle Farm) is especially well-suited to toddlers and a wonderful spot for beachcombing if you don't mind the smell of kelp beds. The rocky beach is nicely sheltered from the wind.

TENTING AREA TO GRANDMA'S BAY AND THE RUCKLE FARM

Our rating: Moderate

Distance: 2 km (return)

Time: 1 – 1.5 hours (return)

Elevation change: No significant elevation changes, though there are ups and downs

Our favourite family walk is the trail beyond the tenting area to Grandma's Bay and then on past the Ruckle Farm.

Follow the gravel path through the tenting area until you have passed the last of the tent sites. You'll find a pretty path that leads around the corner and then along rock outcrops and through groves of arbutus and Garry oak. Small children need an adult hand; there are steep sections, and the path is on a high rocky ledge with a long drop to the water below.

Continue on the gently winding trail (look for orange reflectors) which leads down to Grandma's Bay. Take the wooden staircase down to the bay, where there is a rocky beach decorated with beds of slippery kelp and lengths of seaweed ropes. Crabs and purple and orange sea stars abound. There is a homemade swing at the foot of the staircase, and it is good fun to twirl out over the water.

To resume the walk, climb the stairs and carry on through the woods up a short slope. You will see the rough-hewn fence and the fields of the Ruckle Farm ahead of you. If your timing is right, you can stand

The rope swing at Grandma's Bay

on the rails of the fence and see the sheepdog guiding the herd out of the field. Our children loved this!

The trail goes alongside the fence, and then past several historic buildings that were part of the Ruckle family homestead. Walk around the homestead and see the heritage barn, milk house, forge, machine shop, and pig sty.

There are outhouses located near the barn. To return to the tenting area, walk along the road back up towards the parking area.

RUCKLE FARM HOUSE TO BEAR POINT TO BEAVER POINT

Our rating: Easy

Trail distance: 3.5 km (loop, return)

Time required: 2 – 2.5 hours (return)

Elevation change: No significant elevation changes

This trail starts behind the driveway of the occupied farmhouse across the road from the heritage farm area. It is a beautiful walk through a lush and open woodland of cedar, salal, swordferns, and slugs.

Head over a stile and through the woods behind the house. After about 100 m, the trail goes down a slight hill and into an area where it seems logging has taken place. Here you will see orange trail markers that lead you to the right through the cut area and into an open field. Look for a marker in the field and a sign. At the sign (which faces away from you and marks the trailhead behind you), turn left and follow an unused grassy road that will lead you back into the woods. Continue until you reach the posted park map.

At the map, turn right and follow the trail down the hill. At this point the trail follows the contours of the sheep farm; sheep can be glimpsed in the fields on the right. The trail passes through a grove of old-growth cedar, then meanders through fields and woodland as it circles the edge of the farm. Continue walking until you reach another park map, then turn right through the woods and up a gentle slope.

Here there is another stile to cross, and the trail carries on through second-growth and open forest towards the water, that you can see ahead of you through the trees. At the park map go down the hill and along a bluff that is two to three metres above the beach below. Eventually you will reach an open meadow and then a promontory (Bear Point) with a gentle slope to a rocky beach in a wide bay —a perfect place for a picnic!

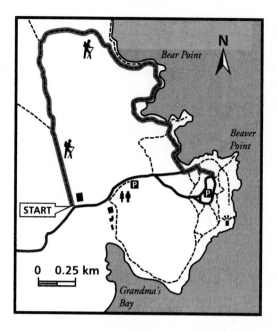

The trail continues through woods and follows the shore through arbutus groves. There are numerous beaches to stop at along the way, though access at Bear Point is best. This part of the trail is steeper and more full of roots—toddlers will need help. At the next headland, the trail turns inland, down into a gully, across a bridge, and up the other side. It then continues past sheltered bays. When you reach the park map, keep left and continue another 750 m to the beach near the Beaver Point day-use area.

To return to the tenting area, cross the road and follow the trail uphill—or follow the Beaver Point trail in reverse (described below).

TENTING AREA TO BEAVER POINT

Our rating: Easy

Trail distance: (from lighthouse) 1 km (return)

Time required: 40 minutes – 1 hour (return)

Elevation change: No significant elevation changes

Walk to the lighthouse. In the meadow just behind the lighthouse, you will see a trail leading through a gap in the trees. The trail goes up a gentle slope along a rocky clearing and into the forest. This trail is hard to follow in the spring because the grass has not grown enough to make it clear, but if you look carefully, you can see a worn area through the trees and meadows as the path follows the contours of the coastline through the forest and rocky outcroppings.

Lots of outcroppings for budding rock climbers to tackle

Take time to sit on the rocks overlooking North Pender and Prevost islands, with Mayne Island peeking out from behind. The trail continues back into the woods and follows a gentle slope uphill. In the spring this area is carpeted with purple violets and a sprinkling of fawn lilies.

Just before arriving at the day-use area, you will pass a park map and a sign pointing to the Beaver Point viewpoint. This view is spectacular and is a less busy option than the day-use area for a picnic. If you do not go to the viewpoint, turn left at the park map and continue to Beaver Point.

At Beaver Point, you will come out near the day-use area parking lot. Follow the trail down a hill, then cross the paved road and you'll see picnic tables. This is a good spot to sit and have some lunch or a snack. Look for a sign marking the trail to the beach. Follow a steep but very short trail to a small sheltered bay with a pebbly beach, a great spot for looking at intertidal life. Return the same way you came.

Bad-weather planning

Camping at Ruckle isn't wilderness camping; civilization is just a short drive away. If it's a soggy day and too wet to be outdoors for long, it's easy enough to drive over to the village of Ganges and poke around the shops, go for a hot chocolate in a café, or even hang out in the public library (open generally 10 a.m. – 4 p.m., closed Sunday). Ganges' Saturday market, with its local artists, farmers, music, and theatre is always fun. Open April through mid-October, from 8:30 – 3:30ish, at Centennial Park.

What you might see

Along the headlands and in the bays, you may see sea lions, mink, river otter, or even porpoises and killer whales. In the woods, look for grouse

First Camping of the Season

It's been too long since we last escaped. But we remember the smell of long grass wet with dew, and the water deep blue against the pale morning sky. It will be so good to be away. We pack our tent, choose our favourite camping food, and meet our friends at the Saltspring ferry lineup.

On this cool morning, the ferry ride seems to lend a particular west-coast drama to our adventure. Kari, Rowan, Elena, and I huddle behind the thick rope that stretches like a gate across the bow, our feet firm on the ribbed steel platform. A mist hangs low around the islands, where evergreens hug rocky cliffs. With the wind whipping our hair, we look for lighthouses as we navigate around the yellow buoys in the strait. Michael, Joseph, and Lisa miss this sight in favour of reading magazines in the warmth of the cars.

There is a light rain falling when we arrive at the trailhead. The children lead us down the path to the tenting meadow, and we find a beautiful spot overlooking the water. Graciously, the rain lets up, we spread out our gear, and soon three tents sit in a neighbourly circle. Elena and Rowan eat lunch like hummingbirds, coming in occasionally for a mouthful, then buzzing away, playing a chasing game that involves a lot of running and silliness. It is good to be here.

(often walking along the hedgerows near the farm) and black-tailed deer. Birds commonly seen include cormorants and eagles.

What to bring

- A frisbee or a ball is ideal for the open spaces near the tenting sites and at the farm.
- Rowan always brings a rope, which is a wonderfully adaptable prop for all kinds of imagination games (bring thick rope only, for safety reasons).
- Shoes with good non-slip soles (water slippers are great) for exploring rock shelves and tide pools.

9 OVERNIGHT
SIDNEY SPIT MARINE PARK
GULF ISLANDS NATIONAL MARINE PARK RESERVE

Expansive, shady beach on the east side of Sidney Island

Our rating: Easy

Distance: 1 km (one-way)

Time: 20 – 30 minutes (one-way)

Elevation change: No significant elevation change

Biogeoclimatic zone/features: Coastal Douglas-fir: forest, meadow, spit, ocean beach, intertidal zone

Land status: National marine park reserve

Best time to go: May to September. The park is open from May 15 to September 30. To make the most of your overnight, go when it's warm. A warm spring or early fall weekend is ideal; there will be fewer visitors than in summer's high season.

Fees: Bring cash for camping fee (self-registration) and for parking in Sidney. Call 250-654-4000 for current camping fee information.

Sidney Spit is an effortless getaway to an island that can only be reached by boat or kayak. A wide, level path leads from the ferry wharf along

Kayaking is the ideal mode of transportation for a trip to a marine park. To reach the park by kayak, launch from the beach next to Beacon Wharf. From there you can paddle straight across Sidney Channel to a small sandy beach just past the private dock (southwest of the public wharf). This beach is perfect for kayak landings, and you'll come ashore at the tenting area. If your child is too young to kayak, try having one parent arrive by kayak, while the rest of the family takes the ferry. Switching roles for the return trip will give both parents a welcome solo stint as well as the pleasure of a family outing.

the edge of the forest to the tenting area, which is bordered by a large meadow. There are expansive, flat, sandy beaches on the north and south sides of the island, with beautiful views and warm shallow waters perfect for wading. Families can beachcomb and splash all day, then sleep under starry skies, seeing the lights of passing ferries and hearing the occasional hum of little boats.

How to get there

Distance from Victoria: 20 km

Driving time: Allow 30 minutes driving plus a 20-minute passenger ferry ride.

Bus: #70 (takes you to Beacon Ave and 5th Street). Call Busline at 250-382-6161 for schedules.

Sidney Spit Marine Park is located on Sidney Island, about five km offshore from the town of Sidney. If driving from Victoria, take Highway 17 north to Sidney. Turn right onto Beacon Avenue at the main Sidney exit. Follow Beacon Avenue until you reach a deadend (you'll see Beacon Wharf in front of you). You may wish to drive onto the wharf and unload gear, then go back and park.

Pay parking (coins needed) is located near the marina. Free parking is available at Iroquois Park behind the city information booth on Lochside Drive, about six blocks from the ferry

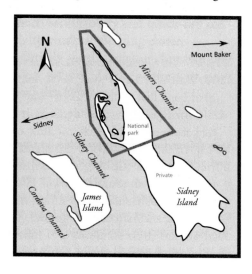

Sidney Spit Marine Park

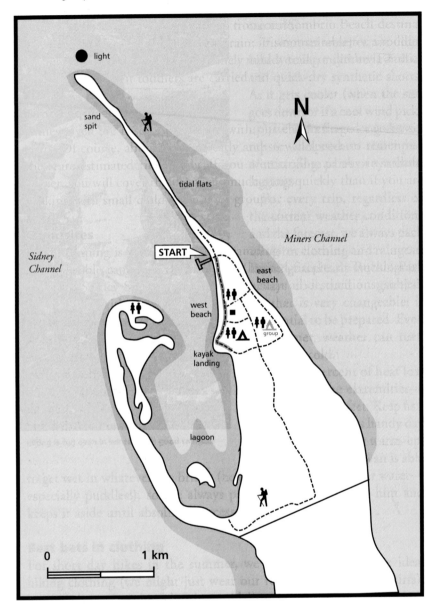

dock. You must phone ahead to Sidney City Hall at (250) 656-1184 and leave your vehicle make and your licence plate number.

From May to September, a small passenger-only ferry leaves from Beacon Wharf for Sidney Spit daily at regular intervals. Sailing time is approximately 20 minutes. On the wharf you will find a sign for the ferry, with sailing times and rates. There is a small gate with a metal gangplank that will go down when it is time to board the ferry. Call Alpine Transport at 250-474-2448 for ferry information.

Nearest facilities
Telephone: Sidney
Gas: Sidney
Groceries and supplies: Sidney
Hospital: Saanich Peninsula Hospital, 2166 Mount Newton X Road, Saanichton (access limited by ferry schedule)
Park services available: Staffed ranger station on the island from May to September

About Sidney Spit
This beautiful marine park is named for the long, narrow sand spit pointing northwest like a bony finger between the waters of Sidney Channel and Miners Channel.

The Coast Salish used Sidney Island as a summer camp for thousands of years. They called the spit "Sktamen" ("submerged by the waves"). They told the legend of a mink named Mutcha who was transformed by the spirit god Swanset into a land mass. The long sand spit of the island was the mink's tail and the beaches its belly and back.

In 1859, the island was named Sidney Island by Captain G.H. Richards after a surveyor friend. From 1906 until 1915, the Sidney Brick and Tile Company operated on the island and employed up to 70 men; the bricks helped build the Empress Hotel. The northern part of Sidney Island became a provincial marine park in 1961, and in May 2003 became part of the Gulf Islands National Park Reserve of Canada. The southern portion of the island is private land.

Trail details
FERRY WHARF TO THE CAMPING AREA
When the ferry pulls into the public wharf on Sidney Island, you will see a long wooden walkway where private boats may be moored. Beyond this is a silvery bridge that leads to a provincial-park picnic area, with cedar tables and firepits. If your timing is right, you may find several large wheelbarrows parked here that you can use to transport gear to the tenting area.

A shady trail beneath a canopy of Douglas fir and arbutus trees begins just behind the picnic area. There is a short (50 m) slope to climb, but once you are at the top, the rest of the gravel trail is level, wide, and well marked (it is actually a road). After just a few minutes, you will see a turnoff to the left, and some outhouses. The left-hand trail goes to the east beach. Keep right for now—it's an easy 30-minute walk to the tenting area.

If you've got two adults with packs full of food, tents, and other gear, children aged two and up can walk most of the way themselves (although the pace will likely be slowed considerably; count on up to 45 minutes). With babies and toddlers, you might want to have one adult carry the child to the camping area while the other adult brings in the gear, making two trips if necessary. It usually takes us at least an hour to unload from the ferry, get our gear together, and make one trip to the camping area.

Camping area

When you reach the camping area, you will see numbered picnic tables in a several locations. There are sites near the water, in a sheltered meadow behind the outhouse, and on the bluff, surrounded by swaying golden meadow grasses. The area can accommodate up to 30 tents; according to the park operator, no one is turned away for lack of space. There is a water tap between the meadow and bluff sites, and another at the water-view sites. Walk around until you find the spot that seems best. This area has been well used and can sometimes be tired-looking. Don't worry! The beaches are just a short distance away and they are glorious.

There is a private wharf near the water-view sites, and the water's edge is littered with piles of red bricks—evidence of Sidney Island's brief industrial activity (if you have arrived by kayak, this is most

Main camping meadow at Sidney Spit

> **Outhouses.** Up the hill from the ferry dock and at the tenting areas.
>
> **Water source.** Water taps, located at camping area. The water has a high sodium content and tastes terrible. It's fine for washing, but bring plenty of your own bottled water for drinking.
>
> **Food storage.** Store food in secure containers well away from your tent.

likely where your boat will be tied up). This is not a good place for young children to play because the bricks are sometimes splintered and have many sharp edges, but our older children have enjoyed "paddling" the kayak here. We tie the kayaks to a length of rope, and they float around in the calm lagoon waters.

Day trips

TENTING AREA TO EAST BEACH

Our rating: Easy

Distance: 1 km (one-way)

Time: 20 – 30 minutes (one-way)

Elevation change: No significant elevation change

The east-facing beach is our favourite place to be on the island. There are great expanses of flat sand, salt marshes, and an outstanding view of the San Juan Islands and Mt. Baker. It is more private than the beach just next to the tenting meadow and well worth the short walk.

At the edge of the tenting area, near the water tap, you will find two trails heading inland through the meadow. Take the left-hand trail (the other is the lagoon trail, which crosses the width of the meadow and goes into the forest on the south end of the island— eventually taking you out to the peninsula that encircles the lagoon).

After a few hundred metres, you will pass the designated group-camping area and a covered picnic shelter. Behind the group-camping area, the trail turns left. You will be walking through mixed forest on a ridge high above the east beach. When you reach a T-intersection, go right (left takes you back to the ferry-wharf trail). You will find stairs leading down to the beach itself. At low tide, flat sands stretch out 75 m, with tide pools and ridges littered with shells, twigs, and seaweed, perfect for building sandcastles or digging holes. The magnificent arbutus trees provide generous canopies, just right for spreading out the picnic blanket and keeping food out of the sun.

Twilight at Sidney Spit

Keep in mind that this side loses the sun in the late afternoon and can be quite cool on a windy day. Bring a windbreaker. It's a great spot for kite flying! For late afternoon and evening sun, or in windy weather, try the more sheltered west-facing beach near the tenting area.

TENTING AREA TO LAGOON
Our rating: Moderate (because of time required)

Distance: 4.5 km (return)

Time: 2 hours return (+ up to 3 hours for lagoon hook)

Elevation change: None

This is an easy but surprisingly long walk on flat, undemanding trails. From the camping area, walk towards the group-camping site, across the bluff and open field. At the edge of the wood, turn right at the trail marker. At this point the trail is a wide gravelly path through cedar, bigleaf maple, and pine. It is cool and open with little elevation. Watch out for the stinging nettles on either side.

The trail passes a meadow on the left and goes through a fence, continuing for another 500 m until it reaches the park boundary. You can't miss it—there is a high chain-link fence and a big sign. At the boundary, turn right (if you were to turn left you would find yourself at a cliff edge). Towards the ocean the trail becomes steep, but only for a short distance of 15 m—just enough to make you breathless on the way up. The path opens to a log-filled beach on one side, and on the other, short but sharp-edged grass that would be hard to walk across. Take the log-filled side of the beach and wander at leisure along the lagoon hook (no marked trail).

Around the lagoon are tidal pools, log jams, and small gravelly beaches. It is a good spot for bird watching—we have seen kingfishers and swallows—

or for picnicking on a sunny day. At low tide, the lagoon is muddy and full of broken bricks; we found it unsafe for walking. If you have a boat, you can explore the lagoon at high tide.

WEST BEACH

This beach borders the trail that takes you from the wharf to the camping area, facing the town of Sidney and Vancouver Island. From the tenting area, it is literally steps away. More sheltered than the east beach, the west-facing beach has big barnacle-covered rocks, gently sloping fine-sand banks, views of shimmering water dotted with pleasure craft, and glimpses of the Sidney Spit dock. This beach is usually busier than the east beach because of its proximity to the wharf and the camping area.

SPIT TRAIL: FERRY DOCK TO LIGHTHOUSE

Our rating: Easy
Distance: 4 km (return)
Time: 2 – 3 hours (return)
Elevation change: None

Start from the ferry dock and take the spit trail to the navigation light at the end of the spit—at least two hours round-trip, at an adult's pace. Children will enjoy going barefoot in the fine white sand. There is lots of driftwood, fun for imagination play. On hot sunny days, remember that there is no shade. Bring hats.

Bad-weather planning

Of course, you can put on raingear and explore beaches in the rain, but you can't be out there all day. When you want to be dry, you can go to the group-camping area (directly east of the family camping area and towards the east beach trail). If no groups are using it, sit under the large covered shelter and sip hot chocolate.

If foul weather has you thinking you might want to shorten your stay, remember, the last ferry leaves in late afternoon.

What you might see

In the early evening and sometimes during the day, children will be delighted to see fallow deer in the field near the tenting area. These are not indigenous, but were introduced to James Island from England nearly a century ago. They swam to Sidney Island in the 1960s. Unfortunately, they have had a devastating effect on the native-plant communities on the island, and present an ongoing resource management challenge.

The marshy pond near the meadow tent sites is home to Canada geese. We have been treated to a parade several times a day as the geese walked in single file past our tent site up to the pond and back. Sidney Spit is located on the edge of the Pacific flyway (bird migratory path). Look for majestic herons on the spit or perched high up in the branches of alders.

Look also for Dungeness crabs and red-rock crabs along the salt marshes on the east beach side of the island. Children will find all kinds of wonderful shells on the island's beaches, including horse clam, pacific littleneck, moon snails, and limpets.

What to bring
- Beach toys like pails, shovels, little boats, beach balls or frisbees, etc.
- Kites are wonderful on windy days.
- Bottled drinking water.
- Allergy medication: Sachiko's daughter had an allergic response to the fresh-cut meadow grass that surrounds the tenting area. If anyone in your group has pollen or grass allergies, make sure you bring the appropriate medication.

Watercolour Sky

Twilight. Soft pinks paint the sky in watercolours. We sit on a bank of golden grasses and gaze out across the gently moving waters. There are pinpoints of light dancing on the waves, cast our way by passing ferries. We sigh, and are quiet. The summer air is fragrant, filled with scents of salt water and the lingering warmth of a sunny afternoon.

"Shall we sing?" asks little Elena.

Our acappella voices rise and fall. We sit side by side, each of us looking into the fading sunset, lost in our own thoughts, happy in the sharing of our songs.

OVERNIGHT
SOMBRIO BEACH
JUAN DE FUCA PROVINCIAL PARK

A rock shelf marks the beginning of the final stretch of East Sombrio

Our rating: Easy

Distance: 250 m on trail and up to another 1 km on beach (one-way)

Time: 30 – 40 minutes (one-way)

Elevation loss: 50 m

Biogeoclimatic zone/features: Coastal western hemlock: forest, ocean beach, intertidal zone

Land status: Provincial park

Best time to go: Early spring and early fall. Sombrio has something to offer every month of the year, but best of all are the times when grey whales visit the bay.

In the fall the whales migrate south to breeding grounds in Mexico, and in the spring they return to Sombrio on their way north to Arctic feeding waters. Summer weekends at Sombrio can be spectacular, but are often crowded. If your family is hardy, winter camping can be fun, but is always wet.

Fees: Day-use parking fee. If camping, parking included in camping fee (self-registration). Cash only. For current fee information, visit the BC Parks website (listed at the back of the book).

Sombrio Beach

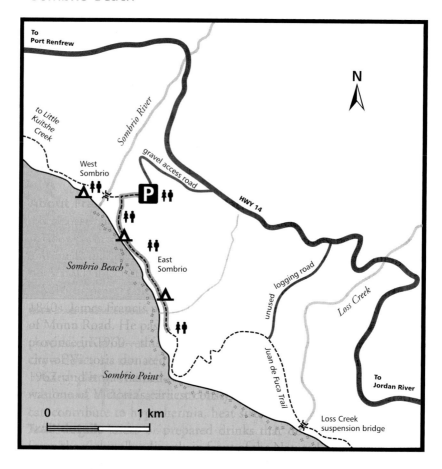

Sombrio Beach is one of the easiest overnight getaways on the west coast of southern Vancouver Island. Its long crescent shape encloses a bay in which whales, seals, and other wildlife feed off kelp beds. Surf crashes wildly on the shore. The beach itself is made up of smooth rocks, sand, and rock shelves. Tents nestle among fantastic piles of driftwood at the high-tide line, and behind the beach are remnants of the old-growth forest that once flourished on the west coast of the island. Sombrio Beach is part of the Juan de Fuca Trail system and offers day-hiking to both the east and the west.

How to get there
Distance from Victoria: 95 km
Driving time: 2.5 hours

From Victoria, take Highway 1 towards Duncan. Exit at the Langford overpass and drive through Langford on the Veterans Memorial Parkway until you reach the intersection for Highway 14. Turn right towards Sooke. The turnoff to Sombrio is 24.5 km past Jordan River.

After Jordan River, the road turns inland. The next section, with its many winding turns, can be difficult for travellers who are susceptible to car sickness. As you approach the turnoff there is a provincial park sign on the right-hand side of the road indicating: "Sombrio Beach 400 metres," but no sign at the turnoff itself, which is on your left. Follow this steep and very rough gravel road for 2 km to the gravel parking lot.

Note: Jordan River is a favourite place for a pit stop on the way to Sombrio Beach. As you approach the bridge crossing Jordan River, turn left into the gravel parking lot along the shore. Here there are outhouses, and you can get out of your car to stretch and watch surfers and kayakers brave the icy waves. On the far side of the bridge, on the inland side of the road, is a small restaurant that sells takeout food.

Nearest facilities

Telephone: Jordan River

Gas: Sooke

Groceries and supplies: Sooke, French Beach (Mini-Mart just before the turn off to French Beach Provincial Park)

Hospital: Victoria General, 1 Hospital Way. There is an ambulance station at Port Renfrew that responds to 911 calls and arranges transport to Victorial General Hospital.

Parks services available: BC Parks staff patrol the beach in high season

About Sombrio Beach

Though some may think of the west coast of Vancouver Island as wilderness, the Pacheenaht people have lived and fished in the area for thousands of years. They were a whale-hunting people who spent their summers living in coastal villages along what is now the Juan de Fuca Trail, and their winters in the shelter of the inland forests. Midden mounds are evidence that Sombrio Beach was once a village site. The area was rich in resources, and the Pacheenaht ate from over 200 different plants and animals and made over 150 different medicines from the abundant forest. The Pacheenaht believed that the "weatherman rock" on the beach warned of storms.

Settlers and pioneers arrived in the area in the late 1800s and began logging the coast. The name Sombrio was derived from the

Fantastic volcanic rock and pools to explore

Spanish word for "shadow," perhaps because of the shadowy canyon of Sombrio River.

When we first moved to Victoria years ago, there were families living as squatters on Sombrio Beach—some had been there nearly 20 years. When the land was designated a provincial park in 1994, these people were asked to move on. Some remnants of their lives on Sombrio remain.

The Juan de Fuca Marine Trail stretches 47 km along the west coast of Vancouver Island, from China Beach to Botanical Beach; Sombrio is one of four entrances to the trail.

Trail details

At the edge of the lower parking lot, you will see a sign with trail and wildlife information and parking fee boxes. A few metres from the trailhead are outhouses. Follow the crushed-gravel trail down the hill through second-growth forest; it is wide and well graded, but a little steep. It is certainly easier to get to the beach than return to the car, especially for small children or parents carrying infants. Give yourself up to 15 minutes to cover this 250 m.

Keep going until you reach two signs—one indicating "East Sombrio 1.5 km," the other "Kuitshe Creek 4 km."

There are camping areas on both East and West Sombrio, but we prefer the east because it is more suitable for families; it is sandier, has fantastic volcanic rock formations and great tide pools, and you can set up your tent up on the beach. It is also farther from the trailhead, and tends to be quieter.

The West Sombrio tent sites are wooden platforms at the forest's edge, mostly hidden from view by high shrubs. There is no sandy beach

> **Outhouses**. There are outhouses in several locations: at the trailhead
> (two), where the East Sombrio trail from the parking lot reaches the beach,
> 250 m down the beach towards East Sombrio; at the far end of East
> Sombrio; in the forest where the Juan de Fuca Trail comes down towards
> the beach; and at West Sombrio, where Kuitshe Creek trail meets the beach
>
> **Water source**. There is a small stream near the far end of East Sombrio.
> During wet seasons additional small streams cross the beach and you
> can fill your bottles directly from them. Filter or boil any water collected
> from the area.
>
> **Food storage**. Hang food at night in the trees behind the beach. We have
> sometimes hiked food back up to the car in the evening, but it makes for a
> long walk.

(it's large cobbles and boulders), and beach access to East Sombrio is
cut off by the mouth of the Sombrio River. To reach the West Sombrio
sites, take the "Kuitshe Creek" fork of the trail and cross the Sombrio
River suspension bridge (about 250 m to the tent sites).

To reach East Sombrio, take the left-hand trail. As you approach the
beach, you will enter a remnant of the old-growth forest—giant trees
tower above the trail. Once you are at the beach, head left and walk
along cobbles and sand (this can be slow going).

You can tent anywhere along the beach, from where the trail meets
the ocean to the far end of East Sombrio (1 km). It is worth the longer
walk to the far end of the beach. Around the corner, beyond a small
rock overhang, there is a smaller, sheltered bay. The actual sign indicating East Sombrio is in a clearing in the forest just behind this last
stretch of beach. To find it (and the outhouse), look for an orange
marker ball in the trees, near a large bleached log jutting out across the
sand.

East Sombrio camping area

There are no designated tent sites at East Sombrio, but enough people
have put tents up over the years that it is not hard to find a spot where
the beach stones or sand have been flattened down. Remember to put
your tent as far back as possible from the high-tide line—the tide can
rise up right to the forest's edge, depending on the time of year. Look
for the highest point where seaweed has been thrown up in a line along
the beach, and place your tent well above this line (there are tide tables
posted at the trail sign near the farthest East Sombrio outhouse).

Day trips

The beach itself is often all the trail we need. There are thousands of interesting rocks and driftwood logs, and at low tide, you can walk on the rock shelves dotted with tide pools. We spend many hours creeping slowly from one pool to another, inspecting anemones, sea urchins, corals, sea stars, crabs, limpets, and much more. Be aware of the tide when walking on the rock shelves, and remember that rocks can be extremely slippery in rainy weather.

EAST ON THE JUAN DE FUCA TRAIL TO SOMBRIO POINT

Our rating: Difficult (steep, very wet and muddy, exposed cliffs—impossible for toddlers to walk on their own, and because of drop-offs, focussed attention and caution is necessary. Even some older children may find it too challenging).

Distance: 2 km (return)

Time: 1.5 hours (return)

Elevation change: No significant elevation changes. The trail has some steep sections.

To hike east on the Juan de Fuca Trail, walk to the far end of East Sombrio and look for an orange marker ball in the trees. You will have to scramble up the bank behind the beach onto the side of the hill, where there is a trail map and, further up, an outhouse.

Follow the trail behind the outhouse, heading up the hillside. The trail is heavy going, winding constantly up and down in the forest, loosely following the contours of the coastline. It is mostly very soft, muddy, and narrow—single file only over large tree roots and steps made with log supports. It can be exciting and fun, and is a good workout—lots of gnarly roots and branches to crawl over and under, boardwalks to cross, and big stretches of oozy mud, which provide numerous opportunities to teach navigation-through-mud techniques!

About 20 minutes from the outhouse, the path descends as a narrow rocky cove comes into view, with glimpses through the trees to a waterfall spilling down the rock wall opposite. The trail crosses a metal bridge that spans a stream flowing out into the rock channel, then climbs back up the hill on the other side.

Log staircase on trail to Sombrio Point

Looking back in the direction you have come, you can see splendid, sweeping views of Sombrio Beach.

The trail moves away from the cliffs and back into the forest. Just before the 27-km marker is a long staircase, each step hand-hewn into an enormous fallen tree trunk—very cool (and also very slippery in wet weather). As you head back towards the cliff edges, with the pounding surf below, some delicate footwork is required (nervous parents may not breathe easily, as there is a steep drop-off and no barriers).

At Sombrio Point (unmarked), you'll find a sunny spot where you can sit just below the trail on a rocky ledge and have a snack or picnic, while watching the amazing strength of the ocean churning and spraying against the rocks beneath you.

With small children, we find this is far enough for an enjoyable walk, so we turn around and head back. The trail does carry on and you may choose to go farther. It is possible to reach the Loss Creek suspension bridge as a day hike, if you start early enough. Make sure you take into account the trip back and your children's staying power before taking on too much additional distance.

WEST ON THE JUAN DE FUCA TRAIL TOWARDS LITTLE KUITSHE CREEK

Our rating: Moderate (boulder-strewn beach walk; toddlers cannot walk without assistance).

Distance: 2 km (return)

Time: 2 hours + (return)

Elevation change: None

To walk the first section of the Juan de Fuca Trail west towards Little Kuitshe Creek, first head back towards the parking lot. Where the trail forks just before the final hill to the parking lot, take the trail marked "Little Kuitshe Creek 4 km."

Follow the shady path to a long, metal suspension bridge, which crosses Sombrio River as it comes out to meet the ocean (toddlers will need help with the stairs at the far end). The path follows the river for a few minutes, passes an outhouse at the 29-km marker, then comes out above a boulder-strewn beach just west of the Sombrio River. Nestled in the treeline above the beach are the wooden tent platforms of the West Sombrio camping area.

Before setting out along the beach for your day hike, make sure you have read and understood the tide tables posted on the notice board. There are three points in the first kilometre of beach where access is cut off at high tide. If your timing is bad, you can easily become trapped, even if you have just gone out for an hour's walk.

Looking down the beach towards West Sombrio

Walking on this beach is very slow going for little people, as it requires stepping from boulder to boulder (not recommended in wet weather). But it is a fascinating landscape with much to look at, including the incredible variety of colour, pattern, and texture in the boulders, and the undulating contours of sculpted sandstone cliffs.

When you reach the end of the first long mass of sandstone cliffs, look up and you'll see the orange marker balls in the forest high above the beach. These mark the overland high-tide access route, which looks like a difficult (if not impossible) climb through brush up a 50-m vertical slope to get to high ground.

Where the trail leaves the beach and heads into the forest, another orange marker ball hangs from a tree (not visible until you are quite close). This is a good place to turn around.

The trail carries on another 3 km to Little Kuitshe Creek, but we find that the first 1 km and back is more than enough for young children, unless you set out early in the day and have carefully accounted for the tides.

Bad-weather planning

There are not many options if the weather turns while you are camping at Sombrio Beach. We recommend making sure you have full wet-weather gear before you leave; then you can just sit back and enjoy the rain. If you are too soggy, you can always pack up and head home for the night. We find this a comforting thought!

What you might see

Seals, sea lions, whales, eagles, otters, mink, and all kinds of seashells, kelp, and abundant life in tide pools.

What to bring

- Sturdy shoes suitable for walking on difficult terrain. The beach itself is rock as well, so comfortable shoes with some ankle support are necessary. Hiking boots or running shoes are best.

- Old tennis shoes or aqua socks are essential for walking on the rock shelves at low tide.
- Bear bells to use when walking in the woods. Both black bears and cougars have been seen on the trails in the area.
- Tide charts. Available at outdoors stores in Victoria, Sidney, and Sooke. These charts will be useful if you decide to hike along the Juan de Fuca Trail. They can be confusing, so ask store staff how to use them. They are also available on-line and are posted at the trailhead if you forget to bring your own.
- Matches, fire starter or paper—and marshmallows! Campfires are permitted at Sombrio in certain seasons (depending on how dry it has been). You can collect plenty of driftwood from the beach itself.
- A tarp with ropes to spread over a section of the campsite so that you can sit back and enjoy the rain.
- Binoculars for seeking out whales.

Cut Cedar and Whales

There is something cozy about camping in the rain. The tarp is up and we've spread a blanket down on the rocks so our bums and legs are warm. It is so beautiful at Sombrio Beach. As we walked out of the trees, the crashing of waves hit our ears and the steep sweep of the beach opened up before our eyes.

At this time of year the air is moist with salt, and the green leaves reaching out to the beach from the forest drip slowly. Underneath our tarp we are comfy. We drink hot soup. The hills have clouded in; the mist rises around us, enclosing us in foggy walls. Rowan jumps on the mat and crawls over our legs. We tell him he can go outside after his Dad finishes splitting wood. He waits impatiently, so we sing "Incy Wincy Spider."

As soon as Michael finishes the wood, Rowan agrees to put on his rain outfit and runs to join his Dad. They go to the water's edge and throw rocks in the waves. I see it first, the blowing mist just past the kelp. Grey whales. At the water's edge Michael picks Rowan up so he can see.

Under the tarp we get a little more comfortable and sit back to watch for glimpses of whales, to smell the cut cedar, to see the setting sun peek out from the mist, and to enjoy the evening.

11

LONG WEEKEND
CARMANAH VALLEY
CARMANAH WALBRAN PROVINCIAL PARK

The first section of the trail to the Three Sisters

Our rating: Moderate

Distance: 2.5 km (one-way)

Time: 45 minutes – 1 hour (one-way).

Note: Unless both parents can carry full backpacks and children can walk the entire trail, one parent will have to make two trips (at least 3 hours total) to bring in overnight gear. Or invite adult friends without children to join you, providing more adults to carry gear.

Elevation loss: 120 m

Biogeoclimatic zone/features: Western hemlock: forest, gravel bar, river

Best time to go: April to September. Spring is an especially lovely time, with the added beauty of fawn lilies, trilliums, and other spring wildflowers. Always check trail conditions and weather forecasts before your trip; wet weather can unleash flash floods, causing Carmanah Creek to rise dramatically, and wreaking havoc with sections of boardwalk. Trails may be closed. The park is remote and repairs take time. Current trail conditions and advisories are normally posted on the BC Parks website.

Fees: BC Parks backcountry fee; payment at self-registration box at trailhead. For current fee information, visit the BC Parks website (listed at the back of the book).

A truly magical place to drink deep the sweet air of an ancient temperate rainforest, one of the last remaining on the planet. Surrounded by the trunks of mossy giants and the arching greenery of forest understory, the trail descends towards Carmanah Creek and leads along boardwalks past numerous fallen giants; one section of trail cuts right through a massive trunk, six feet in diameter. Wilderness camping at the Three Sisters is on an expansive gravel bar, right beside the jewel-green Carmanah Creek.

How to get there
Distance from Victoria: 165 km
Driving time: 3.5 to 4 hours (over 2.5 hours from Lake Cowichan to the park)

From Victoria, drive to Duncan. Just north of town, turn off onto Highway 18 towards Lake Cowichan. You can take either the South Shore Road (past Gordon Bay Provincial Park) or the North Shore Road, which passes the tiny community of Youbou, then skirts the length of Cowichan Lake, until you come to "Nitinat Main" (forestry road). Make sure you have obtained a good map of the forest service roads—regular road maps do not show these roads, and they can be very confusing to identify without a good map. The drive is long enough already without getting lost en route.

Follow signs in the direction of Nitinat, until you reach the junction with South Main. Turn left on South Main, towards Ditidaht and Nitinat Lake (turning right will take you towards Bamfield). Follow South Main, bypassing the village of Ditidaht (keep left at the fork where there is a sign for the Ditidaht First Nation). At the Caycuse River Bridge, blue arrows direct you to the immediate right onto Rosander Main, towards the park. Now you start to climb on a rough, mountainous logging road that rises steeply at times, offering views below to Nitinat Lake. As you ascend the ridge, you will see panoramic views across what is, unfortunately, a huge swath of clear-cut forest, to the Juan de Fuca Strait.

Drive with extreme caution!
Carmanah is a remote destination. Access beyond Lake Cowichan is via active logging roads. The road can be hard on people suffering from car sickness. Make sure you're driving a vehicle that has good suspension and can withstand sections of very rough washboard, major potholes, and loose, large chunks of gravel.

The dust can be very bad. On our first trip, we were choking inside our vehicle and unable to open windows because of the enormous dust trails of passing logging trucks. We encountered more than 15 trucks on the way in. On our second trip, in April, the cooler, wetter weather meant dust-free driving. If possible, travel on weekends when, as a rule, there is little or no logging-truck traffic.

Roads can become impassable due to weather. Always check road conditions before setting out because flooding, washouts, and slope failures are not uncommon (road closures are normally posted on the Carmanah section of the BC Parks website). Driving times are variable, depending on the volume of logging-truck traffic. Other tips to remember:

- Make sure you have a backroads atlas or map clearly showing the logging roads we refer to in the driving directions (a regular road map will be totally inadequate).
- Drive with your lights on to increase visibility.
- Always carry a spare tire and emergency equipment.
- Cover all your gear with a blanket or tarp to reduce dust accumulation.
- Drive defensively and yield to all logging trucks (they have the right of way—other vehicles are expected to pull off onto the nearest shoulders).
- Expect to drive at significantly reduced speed.
- Allow extra time for braking and stopping on slippery gravel roads.

Nearest facilities
Gas: Ditidaht (20 km from the park, north end Nitinat Lake)
Groceries and supplies: Ditidaht (snack food), Youbou (convenience stores)
Telephone: Ditidaht
Laundromat: Ditidaht, at the Nitinat Lake Motel
Hospitals: Cowichan District Hospital (Duncan), 3045 Gibbons Road, and West Coast General Hospital, 3949 Port Alberni Highway
Park services: Trail, washroom, and campground maintenance by private park facility operator

About Carmanah
"Carbadah" (Kwaabaaduwa, "as far up as canoe can go") was the name of a Ditidaht village situated close to where Carmanah Creek meets the Pacific. The First Nations history of this area is complex. The present-day Ditidaht are a grouping of formerly autonomous tribes, some from the Nitinat Lake area, others still from the Olympic Peninsula, and others from Diitiida, near Jordan River.

It is said that at the time of the great flood, they came inland and tied their canoes to Kaakaapiyaa (Mount Rosander, near Nitinat Lake), not returning to the coast until a generation later, when they settled at Whyac (Nitinat Narrows) and prospered as a whaling people.

When freight service to the isolated coastal communities was discontinued in the 1960s and roads were constructed, the Ditidaht settled at the north end of Nitinat Lake.

The Carmanah (and adjacent Walbran) Valley is an area of exceptional ecological diversity, part of one of the last temperate rainforests on the earth, with nearly twice as much biomass (the total amount of living matter in a given area) as the incredibly diverse tropical rainforests. The Carmanah Giant is the world's tallest Sitka spruce, and in addition to stands of rare old-growth Sitka spruce (up to 800 years old), Carmanah is also home to ancient red cedars, some up to 1,000 years old.

In 1988, at the age of 26, young conservationist and wilderness lover Randy Stoltmann revisited the Carmanah Valley, intending to document the ancient forests he had first seen six years before. He was shocked to discover that Canada's remaining stands of some of the oldest and largest Sitka spruce in the world were scheduled for clear-cutting in the near future. Randy worked tirelessly on an international campaign calling for the area to be protected, together with the Western Canada Wilderness Committee and other environmental groups who feared a repeat of the massive industrial logging that decimated much of the ancient temperate rainforest of the Nitinat Triangle and Clayoquot Sound.

The lower Carmanah Valley was granted provincial park status in 1990, and in 1995 continued public pressure led to the protection of the upper Carmanah and the Walbran valleys. The 20-km trail system through the upper and lower Carmanah valley was constructed by volunteers organized by the Western Canada Wilderness Committee.

Trail details

TRAILHEAD CAMPING

A few hundred metres beyond the parking lot and trailhead—along a gravel service road that has been closed to traffic—are 11 walk-in tent sites that are convenient for a quick overnight if you arrive at Carmanah too late in the day to do the hour-long walk to the Three Sisters. Each site has a gravel tent pad, picnic table, and firepit. A water pump and outhouses are at the nearby trailhead. There are two bear-hang food caches: one at the trailhead and a second halfway along the campsite area.

TRAILHEAD TO THREE SISTERS WILDERNESS SITE

At the end of the gravel parking lot, just past the trail information display, picnic tables, and outhouses, the first several hundred metres of the trail is along a level gravel road. Look for the signposted "Valley Mist Trail" on the right (the gravel road continues to the left and around a corner to the trailhead walk-in tent sites).

The Valley Mist Trail is a well-maintained, metre-wide gravel path that leads steeply downhill through towering cedars, balsam, and hemlock

Carmanah Valley

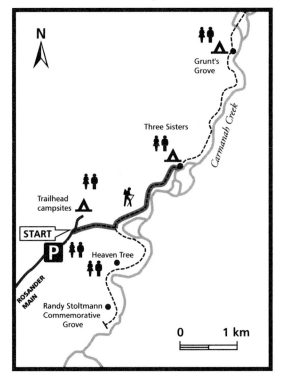

to the junction (km 1.5) of the upper and lower Carmanah Valley trails. Just before the junction is the first section of boardwalk (km 1.2). It leads to a platform at the base of the first of the trail's massive Sitka spruce. This tree is known as the Coast Tower. At the trail junction, you'll find a posted trail map showing the trail routes. Take the Upper Valley Trail towards the Three Sisters. The remainder of the trail to the Three Sisters is mostly wire-covered boardwalk, which is easy walking when dry, but can be extremely slippery when wet, especially where mosses grow on the older sections.

Not far from the junction, you'll descend terraced stairs and pass a hollow stump on the left with an opening large enough for small children to enter, if they are brave enough! It is surprisingly light inside the hollowed-out trunk, and small adults can get head and shoulders inside for a glimpse.

The boardwalk trail is like a bridge passing over a sea of luxuriant rainforest vegetation, with curious and interesting tree forms high overhead, lush undergrowth along the floor, and light filtering in from the adjacent creek valley. Look for numerous trees with abundant "conks"—shelf fungi—growing on their trunks. Close to the Three Sisters, the trail becomes a single-file dirt path as it makes its final descent to the valley floor.

The Three Sisters are three huge Sitka spruce trees growing together. A boardwalk has been built to their base, with a short ladder providing access to an elevated viewing platform nestled in the trunks.

Just beyond the Sisters, a well-worn path is the access point for the wilderness camping area on the gravel bar alongside a gentle bend in Carmanah Creek.

> **Outhouses.** At the trailhead, just beyond Three Sisters, and Grunt's Grove.
>
> **Water source.** Carmanah Creek. Boil, filter, or chemically treat water.
>
> **Food storage.** Hang food; black bears are prevalent in the area. Bear-hang food cache on gravel bar (may or may not be standing straight, depending on previous winter's flood conditions).
>
> **Fires.** No fires are permitted in the valley bottom—ever—no matter what season it is!

THREE SISTERS BACKCOUNTRY SITE

Hikers can set up camp anywhere on the gravel bar on the bank above Carmanah Creek. There are no designated sites; choose a spot you like. Keep in mind that it can become windy and wet, and sites closer to the forest will be more protected. Do not pitch tents along the water's edge; flash floods can turn the gentle creek into a raging torrent in less time than it takes to dismantle your camp.

Day trips

THREE SISTERS TO GRUNT'S GROVE (UPPER VALLEY TRAIL)

Our rating: Challenging (several sections require walking single file across long, narrow deadfalls several metres above the ground, with no hand support)

Distance: 3 km (return)

Time: 1 – 1.5 hours (return) plus time to explore

Elevation change: No significant elevation change, but lots of ups and downs

Beyond the Three Sisters, the Upper Valley Trail becomes more challenging. The walk to Grunt's Grove is a single-file-only dirt trail, with lots of ups and downs and roots to negotiate, and in wet weather, plenty of mud. Older children who like a physical challenge will enjoy numerous opportunities to climb up and over obstacles. Be prepared for detours and minor trail blazing, depending on the time of year.

Where the trail reaches a huge deadfall with two steps cut into the side to allow hikers to scale it, look for the pink ribbon markers signalling that the trail actually goes to the left, *along the top of the deadfall*. Many hikers climb over the deadfall, thinking the trail continues on the other side, but it ends in a dead end soon after.

This is just the first of several natural bridges to cross along the mossy tops of enormous deadfalls. The trail alternately scrambles up short slopes and over and under trees, with some sections of relatively easy walking along level ground in forest carpeted in false Solomon's seal.

Grunt's Grove is marked by a rustic-looking sign, high up on a large tree, next to a narrow trail that leads out of the forest's fringe and onto another of Carmanah Creek's gravel bars. This is the second backcountry camping area, and every bit as pretty as the Three Sisters site. It's a great play area for children, with the creek and its logjams, side pools, and a large gravel bar with some soft, fine-sand areas greened by young spruce seedlings.

Return to the Three Sisters by retracing your steps back along the Upper Valley trail.

THREE SISTERS TO HEAVEN TREE AND RANDY STOLTMANN COMMEMORATIVE GROVE (LOWER VALLEY TRAIL)
Our rating: Moderate
Distance: 6 km to Heaven Tree, 6.6 km to Stoltmann Grove (return)
Time required: 2 hours to Heaven Tree, 3 hours to Stoltmann Grove (return)

From the Three Sisters, go back to the junction of the Upper and Lower Valley trails. At the junction, keep left on the Lower Valley Trail, which heads downstream along Carmanah Creek. The trail alternates between packed earth and boardwalk. Take care not to walk around the Sitka spruce at the Stoltmann Grove; it damages the vulnerable root system.

Bad-weather planning
The Carmanah Valley is temperate rainforest—a wet climate year-round (350 cm per year). Be fully prepared for heavy rain and ensure you have a leak-free tent and a generous tarp (or two), as well as good-quality raingear and extra clothes for everyone in the group.

Carmanah's stillness and quiet are an antidote to the all the ills of urban living. The rain heightens the natural fragrances of the forest, and often results in moody mists that come down into the valley. If you are well equipped for wet weather, you can relax and welcome the sights and sounds of life in an ancient natural sanctuary.

What you might see
As well as the pillars of the awesome forest cathedral, Carmanah's old-growth ecosystem is home to a rich array of insects, birds, and animals including deer, black bears, and the threatened marbled murrelet.

What to bring
- Full raingear, good-quality tent and tarps
- Tree identification guide
- Road map clearly showing forest service roads to Carmanah

12

LONG WEEKEND
LAKE HELEN MACKENZIE
STRATHCONA PROVINCIAL PARK

Boardwalk tent platform at Lake Helen Mackenzie

Our rating: Challenging (easy walking, but considerable distance with young children).
Distance: 3.3 km (one-way)
Time required: 1 hour + (one-way). Note: Unless both parents can carry full backpacks and children can walk the entire trail, one parent will have to make two trips (at least 3 hours total) to bring in overnight gear. Or invite along adult friends without children, so there are more adults to carry gear.
Elevation change: 100 m. There is a long stretch of gradual uphill going in. Biogeoclimatic zone/features: Mountain hemlock: subalpine forest, lake, river
Land status: Provincial park
Best time to go: June to September. Temperatures can be cool and weather changeable at this high elevation. If you can come during a summer warm spell you'll see the area at its best.
Fees: Backcountry camping fee (self-registration). Bring cash. For current fee information, visit the BC Parks website (listed at the back of the book).

This hike offers easy access to Vancouver Island's alpine zone, with no excruciating elevation gain. Boardwalk and cedar-chip trail leads through beautiful subalpine meadows and forest, passing clear streams, wildflowers, and two large alpine lakes. Boardwalk tent platforms are nestled among evergreens, where in the still morning, the sound of loons can be heard calling across the lake. Families can explore the area on day-trails, or splash and swim in the lake shallows, if the weather is warm.

How to get there

Distance from Victoria: 260 km

Driving time: 3.5 hours

From Victoria, take Highway 1 towards Duncan and Nanaimo. When nearing Nanaimo, watch for Exit 19 before you reach the city, and get onto the multi-lane Inland Island Highway, which bypasses Nanaimo, Parksville, Comox, and Courtenay.

Once on the Inland Island Highway, after you have passed the turnoff for Courtenay, watch for a large well-marked sign for Exit 130 to the Mt. Washington Alpine Resort. Turn left onto the Strathcona Parkway and drive 25 km on an excellent paved road until you see condos on a ridge to the right. Turn left onto Nordic Lodge Road, which leads 1.5 km to a gravel parking lot at the Paradise Meadows trailhead. If you reach Raven Lodge Nordic centre, you have gone 500 m too far.

Note: Don't take Highway 19 to the "Forbidden Plateau Recreation Area." If you go down into Courtenay before heading up to Mt. Washington, you may see a turnoff to "Forbidden Plateau Recreation Area." Don't go this way! A gravel road leads to the now-defunct Wood Mountain ski area. While there is access to other Forbidden Plateau trails, this trailhead is *not* part of Strathcona Park.

Pit stops

We like to drive to Mt. Washington non-stop on the first day, leaving home very early and having breakfast in the car so that we can be on the trail by late morning. On the way out, however, after breaking camp and packing all the gear out, we like to stop and let the children play for a few hours. That way they are (hopefully) full of fresh air and will get sleepy during the drive home. These are two of our favourite pit stops.

Miracle Beach Provincial Park. Drive down from Strathcona Park's alpine meadows, and in minutes you're at the ocean's edge. On a warm summer's day, this is a nice spot to spend the afternoon, so you don't have to travel home in a hot car. Once you are back at the Inland Island Highway, drive about 10 minutes north towards Campbell River. You'll see signs to Miracle Beach Provincial Park. Bypass the campground and head to the day-use area just above the beach, where there are picnic tables, washrooms, and a change room. It's a two-minute walk to the flat, sandy beach.

Kinsmen Park (in Parksville). An hour's drive south of Mt. Washington, this park has a big playground with swings and monkey bars galore, plus a cable pull and a water park—all this right beside Parksville's beautiful, expansive beach. There are plenty of picnic tables for family lunches, and an on-site food kiosk and washrooms.

Nearest facilities
Telephone: Raven Lodge Nordic centre (follow Nordic road beyond the Paradise Meadows parking area)
Gas: Courtenay
Groceries and supplies: Mt. Washington Alpine Resort (services available mid-June to early October only, and hours subject to change)
Raven Lodge Nordic centre: food services and showers
Fireweeds General Store (located on Strathcona Parkway, before you reach Alpine Lodge): groceries and other supplies
Laundromat: Raven Lodge Nordic centre
Showers: Free showers at Raven Lodge Nordic centre
Hospital: Comox: St. Joseph's General Hospital, 2137 Comox Ave.
Park services available: Ranger station approximately 4 km past Lake Helen Mackenzie (along the Hairtrigger Loop Trail). No services. BC Parks does not guarantee that a ranger will be at the ranger station at all times. In case of emergency, it would be easier and faster to hike back out to the trailhead (3.3 km).

About Strathcona Park and Forbidden Plateau
According to First Nations' legend, the Comox people sent their women and children to Forbidden Plateau for safety during an attack by their enemies, the Cowichan. But the women and children vanished, supposedly devoured by evil spirits, and the region became taboo.

Strathcona was B.C.'s first provincial park, created by a special act of the legislature in 1911 and named for Donald Smith, Lord Strathcona. It was he who drove the famous last spike in 1885, marking the historic completion of the Canadian Pacific Railway.

Strathcona Park encompasses 250,000 hectares in the centre of Vancouver Island—a wilderness area of glaciers, mountains, lakes, rivers, and stands of coastal and subalpine forest.

At the easternmost edge of the park, immediately south of the Mt. Washington Ski Resort, the Forbidden Plateau area provides diverse hiking opportunities and beautiful subalpine lakes, meadows, and mountains.

Lake Helen Mackenzie

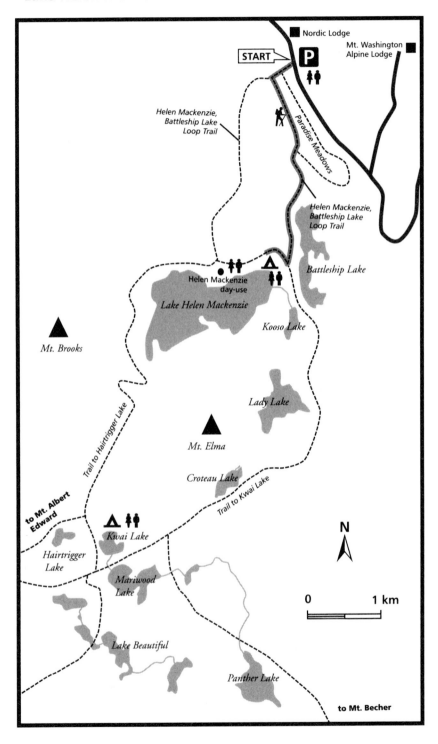

Nordic Lodge

START

Mt. Washington
Alpine Lodge

Helen Mackenzie,
Battleship Lake
Loop Trail

Paradise Meadows

Helen Mackenzie,
Battleship Lake
Loop Trail

Battleship Lake

Helen Mackenzie
day-use

Lake Helen Mackenzie

Kooso Lake

Mt. Brooks

Lady Lake

Trail to Hairtrigger Lake

Mt. Elma

Croteau Lake

Trail to Kwai Lake

to Mt. Albert
Edward

Kwai Lake

N

Hairtrigger
Lake

Mariwood
Lake

0   1 km

Lake Beautiful

Panther Lake

to Mt. Becher

Trail details

PARADISE MEADOWS TO LAKE HELEN MACKENZIE

Most of the trail is either a base of springy cedar chips or cedar boardwalk. The boardwalk is great in dry weather, but could be slick in wet conditions. This would significantly increase walking time.

Start at the Paradise Meadows trailhead in front of the gravel parking lot, where there is a trail map, a self-registration/fee collection box, and an outhouse. The trail descends a moderate slope into a beautiful open meadow carpeted with grasses and wildflowers in the summer. After 0.3 km, there is a turnoff to the left, marked "Paradise Meadows Loop." Continue a few hundred metres further.

A map is posted at the next fork. From here you can go either way to reach Lake Helen Mackenzie. With packs to carry and children to motivate, we prefer the left-hand route, because it is shorter and has nice views of Battleship Lake for much of the trail.

Head left along the boardwalk until you reach another junction. Take the trail on the right, which leads out of the meadow and up a slope—the trail indicator shows that this is the route to Battleship Lake. (If you continue on the boardwalk, you will end up doing a loop through Paradise Meadows back towards the parking lot.)

It's a gradual uphill climb all the way to Battleship Lake. Once there, you will begin the longest two-thirds of the trail, with lots of ups-and-downs along the eastern side of the lake. At the end of Battleship Lake, the left-hand path carries on past Lady Lake and Croteau Lake, to Kwai Lake (a popular backpack destination, central to all the plateau hiking), while the right-hand trail takes you 100 m farther to the Lake Helen Mackenzie backcountry site (and eventually carries on to loop up with the other Lake Helen Mackenzie trail).

LAKE HELEN MACKENZIE BACKCOUNTRY SITE

At the signpost for the backcountry site, a terraced boardwalk leads down past a waste-water site, an outhouse high up on stilts (throne-like! Small children will need adult help to climb the ladder), and metal food-cache boxes. The area is well set up for safe wilderness camping, with a separation of waste, food, and sleeping areas. But the food cache is poorly situated—in hot weather it heats up in the afternoon sun and turns into a stifling oven. Any fresh foods that will be ruined by heat should be packed separately and hung from a sturdy limb.

The tenting area consists of 10 boardwalk platforms nestled among evergreens, all connected by boardwalk paths. Platforms are a generous

> **Outhouses.** At the trailhead, Lake Helen Mackenzie backcountry site, and Lake Helen Mackenzie day-use area.
>
> **Water source.** Lake Helen Mackenzie. Boil, filter, or chemically treat water. Waste water disposal site near outhouse.
>
> **Food storage.** Secure metal food cache provided on-site. If weather is warm, and you have brought fresh foods, don't put them in the metal cache or they will literally bake. Rather, put the fresh items in a sack and hang it out of the reach of animals.

size, with room for stashing gear and extra left over for children to play. If you come mid-week, you may have the whole place to yourself (we did; the children played games running around the boardwalks and onto all the different tent platforms. It was safe and—bonus!—very clean, since feet weren't in the dirt). The boardwalks protect vegetation from being trampled underfoot and prevent some of the wear-and-tear leading to tired-looking sites.

Although the backcountry site is next to the lake, there is no easy lake access. Fronting the tent platforms is a narrow rocky outcrop with a full view of Lake Helen Mackenzie, backed by hills, and the snow of Mt. Elma visible in the distance. The outcrop drops off in a straight vertical 3 – 4.5 m to the lake below, and the lake bottom has large sharp rocks and a steep drop-off itself. When we first saw this, we wondered how much fun this site would be, with nowhere for the children to run around. But after setting up camp, we found good areas for playing, both in the water and out, further down the trail.

Day trips

LAKE HELEN MACKENZIE DAY-USE AREA AND TRAIL

Our rating: Easy

Distance: 1 km (one-way)

Time: 15 – 25 minutes (each way)

Elevation change: None

From the tent sites, return to the Lake Helen Mackenzie trail and head left (away from Battleship Lake). It's an easy 15 minutes to a great play area—a beautiful walk through heavenly green meadows laced with tiny streams, and finally over a small wooden footbridge, where the lake outflow runs clear and deep.

The shallow waters at the tiny "island" (right beside the trail just around the corner from the footbridge) provide an open, safe area with a little bit of sandy beach, perfect for splashing around and adventuring. Children need aqua socks or old runners; the lake bottom is rocky. From here, you can see across the lake to the camping area. Adults can swim in the deeper and colder waters a little further out.

The official day-use area is 10 minutes further. Here the beach is smaller and the water deeper than at the island spot, so it is less suitable for young children. You will likely visit the outhouse here, even if you are based at the other area.

Boardwalk section of the trail to the day-use area

OTHER TRAILS
Our rating: Moderate
Distance: Up to you
Time: Depends on how far you go

If you walk back 100 m to the trail junction at the end of Battleship Lake from the Lake Helen Mackenzie backcountry site, you can day-hike along the Kwai Lake trail (Lady Lake—4 km, return). This is a lovely, easy trail, through varied terrain. In August, you may find carpets of blueberries everywhere. You will have to return the same way you came.

Another option for a day hike is to continue past the day-use area and explore either a section of the trail that goes to Hairtrigger Lake or part of the Lake Helen Mackenzie loop back to Paradise Meadows. Again, return the same way you came.

Bad-weather planning

If it is really wet, options are limited. You've hiked in for an hour and you're at a backcountry site. Here's where planning pays off. With good raingear, a generous-sized tarp, and some inside activities, alternate some outdoor time with a lot of cozy in-the-tent time. Hot chocolate never tasted so good! Although we admit we hate to see the rain starting, we have had some of our best family times when we're all squished in the tent and forced to use some imagination.

You *can* hike out and drive home and be back the same day if it comes to that. Back at the trailhead, if everyone is soaked and feeling miserable, you can take free hot

A cool swim on a hot day near the day-use area

showers at Raven Lodge, then head upstairs to the café for a treat.

What you might see

The plateau is usually covered in lowbush blueberries in late summer. Don't be surprised to see black bears feasting on this abundance. The first time Sachiko hiked the Forbidden Plateau trails, she and Joseph saw six bears in the Kwai Lake area, one of them less than two metres from the trail. There are plenty of aggressive grey jays in the area. They have no qualms about invading your personal space and will brazenly attempt to peck at any food you may be carrying, even if it is in your hands. Some children will be fascinated, but others might be frightened.

What to bring

- Bathing suits or quick-dry shorts and T-shirts in case the weather is warm.
- Bear bells or other noisemakers for everyone in the group; the plateau is home to many black bears.
- Fishing gear: If you can manage to pack it in, the lakes are stocked with rainbow trout and fishing is excellent (a valid B.C. angling licence required).
- National Topographic Series map sheet 92F11 (available at Crown Publications in Victoria for about $10, Tel: 250-386-4636). The map provided on the provincial park brochure (downloadable at the BC Parks website) does not provide adequate detail to get a feel for the contours of the trails.

Sleepless in Strathcona

We didn't want to bring two tents or the big four-man tent—both were too heavy for the long hike in. The plan was for Joseph to sleep outside, but the mosquitoes are unexpectedly ravenous. As a result we are impossibly squeezed into a single two-man tent: one man, one woman, a five-year old girl, and a toddler. Elena is relegated to a little rectangle at our feet, while Joseph, Marin, and I "share" the zipped double bag. Sharing, however, means that Marin is splayed out in the middle and we find our noses pressed into the walls of the tent.

Once she falls asleep, I reason, I'll move her to the side and we'll have more room. But she is tossing and turning. Just as she seems to settle, she's twisting around again. Her little hands are scratching at her head. She turns again. She absently scratches violently at her belly. Why won't she settle down?

Fast forward six hours; it is now 4:00 a.m. I have not slept a wink and am conscious of the ticking sound of my watch. I whisper to Joseph, "Have you slept at all?"

"No," is his flat reply.

Something dawns on me. I rip open the snaps of Marin's sleeper and stare at her stomach. I can't see—it's too dark. I fumble for the flashlight and click the beam on. It's confirmed. Chicken pox in the woods. I lie flat on my back, sigh, and listen to the dawn chorus.

OLYMPIC NATIONAL PARK (WASHINGTON STATE, U.S.)

Destinations 13 and 14 are in Washington State's Olympic National Park.

We are surprised how few of our outdoor-loving friends are familiar with this fabulous park, literally just across Juan de Fuca Strait from Victoria. A short ferry ride away, at the most northwestern point of the continental U.S., Olympic National Park is a World Heritage Site and Biosphere Reserve. This park has it all—stunning alpine hiking, forests, lakes, coast, and rainforest. Hiking trails and wilderness camping areas are generally quiet and uncrowded—the way we love them. And you don't have to drive more than an hour to reach them.

While there are many challenging, multi-day wilderness routes (which we hope to revisit again with older children), there are also suitable destinations for families with young children. We include two of our favourites. They can be done as individual long weekends, or you might like to combine them into a mini-vacation.

History

The heart of the Olympic Peninsula is dominated by the Olympic Mountains and surrounded by lowlands, which were once cloaked in magnificent virgin forests. A rich coastal Native culture existed in harmony with the natural abundance, with an economy based on hunting and gathering that was sustained by salmon and steelhead, shellfish, and game. The archaeological record shows that Native Americans lived on the Olympic Peninsula for over 12,000 years before European explorers arrived in the late 1700s.

A number of distinct bands include the Quilcene ("salt-water people") and Skokomish ("fresh-water people") in the east, the S'Klallam and the Elwha in the north, the Makah (Cape Flattery area), and the Quileute, Queets, and Quinault (in the south). Native cultures of the Northwest coast culture area (northern California to southern Alaska) are considered by anthropologists to be among the most complex and highly developed Native cultures north of Mexico.

In 1855 and 1856, the Native peoples of the peninsula signed treaties, ceding the entire peninsula to the United States, except for the tiny areas they retained as reservations. Today more than 85 percent of the ancient forests have been destroyed by logging.

In 1890, the first proposals were made to give the Olympic Mountains national-park status. Over the next 50 years, parts of the area were protected under a number of schemes, with lands added and deleted in response to lobbying and commercial interests. With the support of President Franklin D. Roosevelt, Olympic National Park was created by Congress in 1938. On several occasions the park was enlarged to include not only the central and western Olympics, but also a large area in the north and southeast, extensions down western river valleys, and a 50-mile coastal strip along the Pacific.

Getting to Port Angeles

Distance from Victoria: 29 km
Travel time: 90-minute ferry ride

Note: Distance and time here is to Port Angeles only. From Port Angeles, you must then drive to trailheads for individual destinations (see Destination 13—Upper Lake Mills, and Destination 14—Rialto Beach).

From Victoria, take the M.V. *Coho* ferry to Port Angeles, Washington. The ferry terminal is in the Inner Harbour just behind the Wax Museum (430 Belleville Street). From May to September there are several daily departures. It is not possible to make reservations, so make sure you call ahead for the advised time of arrival to ensure boarding; tel: 250-386-2202. You might have to pre-park your vehicle overnight.

Ensure you are aware of your health coverage when in the U.S. You should purchase insurance if you do not have any coverage; an unexpected stay in an American hospital can be very costly.

You will need to bring proper identification to cross the U.S. border. Staff at the M.V. *Coho* can advise you of current requirements, or contact the U.S. Consulate in Vancouver.

Olympic National Park Wilderness Information Center (WIC)

600 East Park Avenue, Port Angeles, WA 98362
Tel: 360-565-3100 (fees, permits, reservations and information for backcountry areas).
E-mail: olym_wic@nps.gov (backcountry questions)
Website: http://www.nps.gov/olym/wic/wic.htm

Once in Port Angeles, head for U.S. Highway 101; watch for a sign to the Olympic National Park Visitor Center. Follow Race St. to the Visitor Center. The WIC is located directly behind the Visitor Center.

13 UPPER LAKE MILLS
OLYMPIC NATIONAL PARK (WASHINGTON)

Gravel bar and shallow pools at Upper Lake Mills

Our rating: Moderate (short distance but steep switchbacks)

Distance: 0.6 km (one-way)

Time: 15 – 20 minutes (one-way)

Elevation change: 120 m

Biogeoclimatic zone/features: Subalpine montane: mountain hemlock forest, river

Land status: U.S. national park

Best time to go: Summer or early fall

Fees: National park entry fee (pay at gate), backcountry camping fee (purchase permit at ranger station). For fee information, contact the Olympic National Park Wilderness Information Center (see p. 151).

Located in the Elwha Valley area of Olympic National Park, this very short trail winds down several steep switchbacks through open second-growth forest to the banks of the Elwha River, near where it empties into the head of Lake Mills. A shady bower of bigleaf maples and a sunny gravel bar provide lovely settings for camping beside a deep-green-blue river, against a backdrop of forested hills and mountain peaks.

How to get there

Distance from Port Angeles: 32 km
Travel time from Port Angeles: 25 minutes

Leaving the ferry terminal in Port Angeles, turn left on Railroad Avenue, then right two blocks later at N. Lincoln. Stay in the right-hand lane on Lincoln until you see signs indicating U.S. Highway 101, then keep right and head west on Highway 101 towards Lake Crescent and Forks. About 20 km west of downtown Port Angeles, look for the sign indicating "Olympic National Park, Elwha River" and take the turnoff on your left, just before Route 101 crosses the Elwha River.

After 3 km you will reach the park gate, where there is an entrance fee (approximately US $10; can be paid by credit card). Continue another 3 km to the Elwha Ranger Station. You must purchase a wilderness camping permit (US $5 permit registration, plus US $2 per adult per night) and rent the required bear-resistant food container (by donation; suggested US $3).

To get to the Upper Lake Mills trailhead, drive on past the ranger station and take the first left onto Whiskey Bend Road, a single-lane gravel road that climbs steeply, winding through a canopy of trees high above the Elwha Valley and past the Glines Canyon Dam. It takes about 15 minutes to drive the 7 km to the trailhead, which is just a pullout on the right marked by a small sign. There is space for about four vehicles to park end to end. If you reach the end of Whiskey Bend Road, you have gone five minutes too far.

Nearest facilities

Telephone: Outdoor pay phone at Elwha Ranger Station. You will need U.S. coins, or you can pay by credit card (at an exorbitant rate). Canadian calling cards are not accepted, but if you have a Telus calling card, you can dial 1-800-646-0000 to make calls on your calling card.

Gas: Where Route 101 meets Route 112, 17 km back towards Port Angeles from Olympic Hot Springs Road

Groceries and supplies: Several large grocery stores along N. Lincoln Avenue in Port Angeles (you are not allowed to bring fresh fruits, vegetables, or meat across the U.S. border, so plan to supplement your groceries in Port Angeles). Wilderness camping supplies are available at Brown's Outdoor or Olympic Mountaineering, both on W. Front Street, near the Port Angeles ferry terminal.

Laundromat: On Front Street and on First Street, near the ferry terminal, Port Angeles, or at the Log Cabin Resort, northeast end of Lake Crescent. Tel: 360-928-3325

Showers: Log Cabin Resort (above) or try the Shadow Mountain Campground at the eastern end of Lake Crescent. Tel: 360-928-3043

Hospital: Olympic Medical Center, 939 Caroline St., Port Angeles

Ranger Station: Elwha Ranger Station (Olympic Hot Springs Road). Open mid-June to mid-September. Hours variable. Tel: 360-452-9191

About the Elwha Valley and Lake Mills

"Elwha" is a Klallam Indian word meaning "elk." For thousands of years, the Klallam people lived along the rich watershed of the Elwha River, their lifestyles closely tied to sea-run fish populations. In the late 1800s, pioneers began to establish themselves in the area, many en route to the Alaska gold fields. Two dams were constructed on the Elwha River in the early 1900s to help power logging operations in the area; neither allowed for fish passage. Fish runs were devastated, disrupting the ecosystem of the Elwha watershed. Lake Mills was the lake created by the Glines Canyon Dam in 1927. In 1992, the U.S. Congress required the restoration of the Elwha watershed. The dams are on schedule to be removed in the next several years, restoring over 100 km of rich salmon habitat.

Trail details

TRAILHEAD TO UPPER LAKE MILLS WILDERNESS SITE

From the parking area, the first five minutes is easy walking along a footpath down a gentle slope through an open second-growth forest. The trail then narrows and follows a steep grade down to the banks of the Elwha River. Most of the elevation loss is in the last two-thirds of the trail: five steep switchbacks, single file only, with loose gravelly sections that can be slippery. This trail could be quite difficult in wet conditions. As you descend the last switchback, you will catch glimpses of the Elwha just below you. The trail ends at a flat, sandy bank shaded by bigleaf maples, near the river's edge.

UPPER LAKE MILLS WILDERNESS SITE

"Lake Mills" is a misleading name for this site, as you can't see the lake; you are alongside the Elwha River before it empties into the lake (or at high water, floods and literally becomes part of the lake). There are

> **Toilet facilities.** None. Bury waste 15 – 20 cm deep, at least 100 m from campsites and water sources. Pack out toilet paper. The nearest outhouse is at the end of Whiskey Bend Road.
>
> **Water source.** Elwha River. Boil, filter, or chemically treat water. Or keep a plastic water reservoir in your vehicle and refill as necessary.
>
> **Food storage.** Bear canisters are mandatory. You can rent them from the Elwha Ranger Station for a nominal fee, but call ahead to ensure you get one.

established shaded tent sites under bigleaf maples on the flat, sandy, and sometimes damp river bank, or you can tent out in the open on a soft, sandy spot on the 500-m-long gravel bar, which is exposed when the river is not too high.

To experience the site at its best, come when the water is low and the gravel bar is exposed. It is covered with small willow trees and bordered by shallow pools from the outflow of Wolf Creek.

The resulting open area is perfect for young children; parents can easily sit and sun, while little ones float leaf-boats, splash in warm pools, hunt for fingerlings and frogs, or play in the sand—all in full view. Just behind the gravel bar, look for the beautiful waterfall in a shaded grotto set into the forested slope where Wolf Creek drops 15 m into a small pool.

Contact the Elwha Ranger Station and ask about water levels before you make plans. We have only camped here at low water and would not be so enthusiastic about this site if there were no gravel bar. In our opinion, the site would be closed in too tightly by the river at high water and much less suitable for small children. Once the Glines Canyon Dam is removed (scheduled for 2005 or 2006) and the Elwha flows freely downstream, the gravel bar will be constantly exposed in summer.

Day trips

There are all kinds of day hikes in the Elwha Valley, but the closest and one of the nicest is to Humes Ranch. The trailhead begins five minutes past the Lake Mills trailhead, at the end of Whiskey Bend Road. There is an outhouse at the trailhead.

MICHAEL'S CABIN AND HUMES RANCH ALONG THE UPPER BENCH
Our rating: Easy
Distance: 4 km (return)
Time: 2 hours (return)
Elevation change: No significant elevation change

Upper Lake Mills and the Elwha Valley

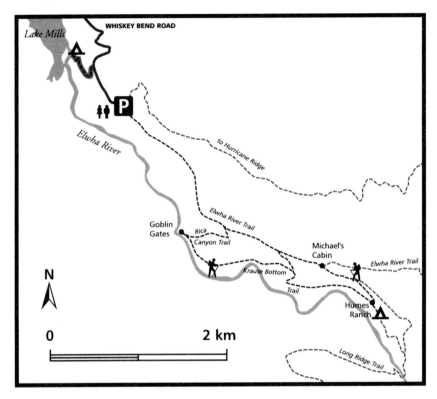

From the trailhead at the end of Whiskey Bend Road, take the Elwha River Trail through open shaded forest along a high bench. Although it's called the Elwha River Trail, you won't actually see the river on this portion of the trail. This is an easy walk and is about an hour in and an hour out—you are on the same trail both going and coming back. At km 3, you will pass Michael's Cabin. It's another kilometre to Humes Ranch, where you might enjoy lunch in the shade of the worn wooden porch of the cabin built in 1900 by homesteading brothers who also guided in the region. You can gaze out over the overgrown meadow as you enjoy a break, then return the same way you came.

There is very little elevation to contend with if you keep to this upper bench trail—unlike the loop trail explained below.

Note: You might also like to do this as an alternate or additional overnight destination. A designated wilderness site is located at the large meadow just below Humes Ranch, and it is a feasible backpack hike in and out for families with young children.

RICA CANYON, GOBLIN GATES, KRAUSE BOTTOM TO HUMES RANCH; A LOOP ROUTE, RETURNING VIA MICHAEL'S CABIN

Our rating: Moderate (some steep sections, narrow, rocky trail, and along ledges very close to river in places)

Distance: 6.8 km (return)

Time: Over 3 hours (return)

Elevation loss: 150 m

For a more challenging day trek, do a loop, taking the steep trail down to Rica Canyon and Goblin Gates, along Krause Bottom, and then up to Humes Ranch and back along the bench trail. It will take you about 1.5 to 2 hours to reach Humes Ranch and an hour to walk back out via Michael's Cabin.

Start out on the Elwha River Trail. At the km 1.6 signpost, turn right at the junction onto the Rica Canyon trail. The trail descends quickly and steeply through an area reforested after a burn, then into open evergreen forest 150 m down to the river's edge. Just before the river is a side trail to Goblin Gates that leads a few hundred metres along a narrow ledge to a sandstone outlook, literally right above the Elwha's whitewater. Here the "gates" of the river force the water to swirl and froth, emerging into deep aqua pools. It is not an easy path for small children. You may want to check it out first before deciding if it's suitable.

Returning from the Goblin Gates side trail, rejoin the main trail, which has views of the river through a lush, luminous forest of Douglas fir, vine maples, and bigleaf maples, carpeted with moss-covered logs and thickets of club moss. About 1.5 km from the Goblin Gates is a junction. The left trail ascends to meet the Elwha River Trail (the one you started out on). Keep right on the Krause Bottom Trail, which heads to Humes Ranch. You will eventually climb up to a small meadow

Make pottery!

Just past the Goblin Gates side trail, near an established campsite, look for a natural pool in a side channel of the Elwha river. You will have to scramble down an eroded bank and over large boulders. The beautiful green-blue waters are deep enough for a very quick and cold swim (for adults). An added attraction is a clay bank, where children will love squooshing in the clay and making shapes and figures that bake quickly on a sunny day when placed on the warm rocks.

above the river, the site of the Humes pioneer homestead.

If you face the cabin, on your left you will see a trail leading out of the meadow and into the forest. This will get you back onto the Elwha River Trail, your return route. Less than 1 km from the ranch, you will pass Michael's Cabin. The final 2.8 km is easy going (keep straight through all intersections) and brings you back to the trailhead and parking lot.

Note: If you think you might like to do the loop in the opposite direction, keep in mind that you will have a steep climb out at the end of your hike, when everyone is tired. We did this the first time we came, and would not do it again.

Bad-weather planning

If you are camping at Upper Lake Mills and it gets too wet, there are a couple of things you might do instead. You might want to move your tent to one of the park's campgrounds, where you won't have to try to get up and down muddy switchbacks. Once back at the beginning of Whiskey Bend Road, try the Altaire campground (turn left; drive for 5 minutes), or the Elwha campground (turn right; less than five-minute drive). There are also very basic cabins at the Log Cabin Resort on Lake Crescent (US $60 or more per night).

You might like to drive to the Sol Duc Valley Hot Springs for a soak. Get back out to Highway 101 and drive about 30 km west, past Lake Crescent, where you can stop in at the Storm King Ranger Station for information and publications about the park. About 3 km past Lake Crescent, at the crest of a hill, there is a sign for Sol Duc Valley Hot Springs Resort. It's another 20 km to the hot springs, which are open 9 a.m. – 9 p.m. May to September (US $3 – $10 admission fee). Hopefully you have packed bathing suits! There's an on-site deli where you can buy snacks.

An option you might like to try early on the day you plan to head home is to drive back to Port Angeles, then up to Hurricane Ridge. As you re-enter Port Angeles on Highway 101, keep going east until you see the signs for the Olympic National Park Visitor Center and Hurricane Ridge. Turn right. The Olympic National Park Visitor Center (open 9 a.m. – 5 p.m.) has interesting interpretative displays and a slide program. From there, you can drive another 20 km straight up into the alpine. There are gorgeous views to Victoria and Vancouver Island on a clear day, but if you are here in the rain, you will see deep valleys shrouded in mist.

From the top of Hurricane Ridge, there are several fabulous day hikes in the alpine. If it is too wet, the Hurricane Ridge Visitor Center (open 10 a.m. – 5 p.m.) has exhibits, a slide program, and a café.

What you might see
In the shallow side waters of the Elwha, look for salmon fingerlings and frogs. The Elwha Valley trails are great places to identify trees.

What to bring
- U.S. cash. for camping and registration fees, although these can normally be paid for by credit card at ranger stations.
- I.D. for the U.S./Canada border crossing. Check with the M.V. *Coho* ferry staff or the U.S. Consulate in Vancouver for current requirements.
- Information about your health insurance coverage. You don't want to have to visit an American hospital without coverage.
- Bear-resistant food containers. If you are planning to get these in the park, call ahead to confirm that hard-sided snap-top food containers are available at Elwha Ranger Station. Otherwise you will have to visit the Wilderness Information Centre in Port Angeles, which is a short detour from a direct route to the Elwha from the ferry terminal. It's simplest to bring your own.
- Maps. You can purchase topographic maps at the Elwha Ranger Station.

Sleeping Under the Stars

"Mama! I see one!"

"Me, too, I see one!"

There, in the blue-purple sky above the silhouette of the mountain opposite, a tiny pinprick of bright light. And then another, and another. The magical map of the night sky. We wait all the long winter for this ... to fall asleep in warm evening air under the stars. We pull our sleeping bags and sleeping pads out of the tent and spread them out on the soft bank. Side by side, we gaze heavenward. Here, the Little Dipper, there the North Star. Is that a shooting star? Or the light from a passing plane? Questions, speculations, stories.

Then the girls grow quiet. Their deep breathing tells us they are in the land of starry dreams. We drink in the stillness and it fills us up.

14

Driftwood giants strewn along Rialto Beach

Our rating: Easy

Distance: 1.6 km (one-way)

Time: 30 – 45 minutes (one-way)

Elevation change: None

Biogeoclimatic zone/features:
Coastal western hemlock: forest, ocean beach, intertidal zone

Land status: U.S. national park

Best time to go: May to September. Be forewarned that this area is one of the wettest in the entire U.S.! Go expecting wet weather, no matter how optimistic the weather forecast.

Fees: Backcountry camping fee (purchase permit at ranger station). For fee information, contact the Olympic National Park Wilderness Information Center (see p. 151).

Rialto Beach is near the Quillayute River, near the Quileute Indian village of La Push on Washington's northwest coast. With surf crashing and enormous silvery wind-bent trees fringing the sand, this easy hike along a cobble beach passes sculptural sea stacks and gigantic piles of driftwood. Set up tents in the shelter of rainforest giants or nestle into a driftwood alcove facing the wild Pacific.

How to get there

Distance from Port Angeles: 110 km

Travel time from Port Angeles: 1.5 hours (plus ferry from Victoria to Port Angeles)

When you leave the ferry terminal in Port Angeles, turn left on Railroad Avenue, then right two blocks later at N. Lincoln. Follow

N. Lincoln until you see signs indicating U.S. Highway 101. Head west on Highway 101 towards Forks.

After just over an hour's drive, and before you reach Forks, turn right onto La Push Road (Highway 110) and continue 12 km. There is a private campground, gas station, and convenience store at the intersection of La Push Road and Mora Road; turn right onto Mora Road. After 4 km you'll reach the Mora Ranger Station next to the national park campground, where you can purchase your wilderness camping permit (US $5 permit registration plus US $2 per adult per night), rent the required hard-sided food containers (by donation), and get a final weather forecast.

The final 8 km is a beautiful drive in any weather, with the otherworldly vivid greens of the coastal forest bordering the road on either side as you travel down a majestic avenue of towering evergreens. Where the Quillayute River meets the Pacific, you turn into the Rialto Beach parking lot.

Nearest facilities

Telephone: Outdoor pay telephone at Mora Ranger Station
Gas: Three Rivers Resort, junction of Mora Road and La Push Road
Groceries and supplies: Convenience store, Three Rivers Resort. Grocery stores in Forks (25 km from Rialto Beach)
Laundromat and showers: Three Rivers Resort
Hospital: Forks Community Hospital, 530 Bogachiel Way, Forks.
Ranger Station: Mora Ranger Station, Mora Road. Tel: 360-374-5460

About Rialto Beach and the Pacific Coastal Strip

Rialto Beach is at the midway point of the 95-km coastal strip of Olympic National Park. This wild coast is characterized by pounding surf, dramatic sea stacks and arches, flat sand and cobble beaches, enormous driftwood piles, and an endless horizon to the west over the grey waters of the Pacific.

The entire coastal strip has been home to Native peoples for thousands of years, from the Makah in the north to the Quinalt in the south. Immediately south of Rialto Beach at the mouth of the Quillayute River is the town site of La Push, home to the Quileute people.

It is possible to do several multi-day hikes the length of the coastal strip, but these are demanding and unsuitable for families with young children. Most beach access points are via trails of varying length, often through very dense coastal forest.

The easiest access to the coast is at Rialto Beach, where a paved road leads to a parking area a few hundred metres from the beach. However,

Rialto Beach

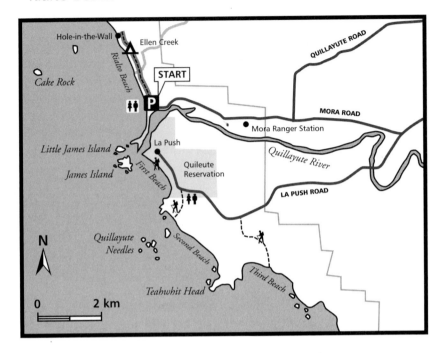

because of the easy access, Rialto Beach sees a lot of visitors, both day hikers and those looking for an easy overnight. Unfortunately, some people do not practise Leave No Trace camping, and it can be disappointing to see what they have left behind. Try to come mid-week, when there will be fewer people; many hikers come on a Friday or Saturday and just stay the weekend.

Trail details

RIALTO BEACH TO ELLEN CREEK

At the far end of the Rialto Beach parking lot, you will see an outhouse building and garbage disposal area. Just beyond this is the trailhead notice board, the self-registration and fee box, and posted tide tables (you can buy your own tide tables at the Mora Ranger Station). You will need the tide information to gauge whether you can safely camp on the beach or should head into the trees. The tide table will also help you plan the best time to explore the Hole-in-the-Wall sea arch, which is only accessible at low tide.

Follow the short, paved path past a picnic area to the beach access. If it is clear, you will see James Island and Little James Island to your left and the flat-topped "Cake Rock" several kilometres offshore to the right.

Head north (right) along the beach. At low tide it is an easy walk along firm, flat sands, but if you are setting off at high tide, you will be walking on cobbles and may have to scramble around mammoth driftwood logs above the high-tide line.

When you reach Ellen Creek, look around to see the narrowest crossing point, unless you are prepared to get your feet wet.

ELLEN CREEK WILDERNESS SITE

No camping is permitted before reaching Ellen Creek, but once you have crossed the creek, you can camp anywhere along the beach or in more sheltered established sites in the trees, all the way up to Hole-in-the-Wall (0.8 km). Mid-week you will probably be able to scope out your preferred spot, but on weekends this is a popular destination and choices may be limited.

The first time we came here, the tide was very low and we camped on the beach in a driftwood nest. However, a second trip coincided with much higher tide levels, and, it being a weekend, the more elevated sites in the trees had already been taken. There was a somewhat anxious wait for the high tide to hit, in order to see whether our planned spot on the beach would be dry or not.

In high season, you will probably have to share Rialto Beach with many other lovers of the wild coast, but the massive bleached drift-

---

Toilet facilities. Flush toilet at parking lot, outhouse in the trees near Hole-in-the-Wall (0.8 km from Ellen Creek and way too far for young children to make it without advance planning!)

Try to time a walk towards Hole-in-the-Wall at a strategic point in your day, so you will avoid having to go to the toilet above the beach in the trees. Undergrowth is dense and vegetation sometimes above an adult's head—very challenging to get the recommended 60 m from campsites and water sources.

If you must go in the trees, dig a hole and bury waste 15 – 20 cm deep, and pack out toilet paper.

Water source. Ellen Creek. Boil, filter, or chemically treat water. The last time we were here, the Ellen Creek water was unappealing. We drew from a portable reservoir filled with Victoria water that we kept in our vehicle.

Food storage. Hard-sided food containers with snap-down lids are mandatory, and can usually be rented for a nominal fee from Mora Ranger Station.

wood up and down the beach creates natural privacy screens, and noise from other people is swallowed by the roar of the surf.

Day trips
ELLEN CREEK TO HOLE-IN-THE-WALL
Our rating: Easy

Distance: 1.6 km (return)

Time: 1 hour (return)

Elevation change: None

This is a wonderful walk for small children. They can run freely along the flat sand and watch oystercatchers swoop down to the water, or admire colourful stones on the beach. Sachiko's two-year-old daughter loved climbing up enormous smooth rocks whose surfaces were miniature worlds of little pools to peer into.

Walk north along Rialto Beach past Ellen Creek. Offshore, you will pass several impressive sandstone sea stacks of all sizes. The largest one, nearly 25 m high, resembles the mountains depicted in some Oriental landscape paintings: tall and thin, coming to a point at the peak, with bonsai-shaped evergreens miraculously growing out the side of solid rock.

Beyond the last stacks, you will see the wide, rocky headland with its graceful, rounded arch known as Hole-in-the-Wall. At low tide, the rocky ledges around and leading into the arch let you explore an amazing sea garden, where you will find crevices and pools filled with pink and green sea anemone colonies, vivid purple and orange sea stars, barnacle colonies, and much more. At low tide, you can walk right through the Hole-in-the-Wall to the other side and see a beautiful view of the Pacific through the frame of the arch.

ELLEN CREEK TO LITTLE JAMES ISLAND
Our rating: Easy

Distance: 2 km (return)

Time: 1.5 – 2 hours (return)

Elevation change: None

Another option for a day walk is to retrace your steps back towards the Rialto Beach trailhead, then go beyond it towards Little James Island. About 0.8 km south of the parking area, there is a man-made rock jetty that sits parallel to the beach, beside the mouth of the Quillayute River. At low tide, you can walk to the jetty and climb up for a higher vantage point on the panorama stretching out 180 degrees in front of you. If you go far enough down the jetty at low tide, you will find a sand spit, which connects to Little James Island. Rock pools at the base of the island are home to lots of intertidal life.

FIRST BEACH (LA PUSH)
Our rating: Easy
Distance: 3.2 km (return)
Time: 2 – 3 hours (return)
Elevation change: None

For another interesting day trip, pack your lunch into a day pack and hike out from Ellen Creek to the parking lot, then drive back to the intersection of La Push and Mora road. Turn right onto La Push Road. It's about 12 km to the village of La Push, on the Quileute Indian Reservation. Park near the Quileute Tribal School. You will see a dirt road leading to the northern end of the beach.

As you reach the beach, to your right is a stone jetty next to the Quillayute River. Just beyond the jetty is James Island. The island's 60-m bluffs served as a fortress for the Quileute when they were attacked by Makah warriors from Neah Bay.

Sea stacks at Rialto Beach

You can walk south along the smooth crescent of sand beach, one of the widest on the Olympic coastal strip, with the quiet roar of big surf in the background. Ahead in the distance are the 25-metre cliffs of Quateeta Head and, to its right, the Quillayute Needles sea stacks. The trail ends at Quateeta Head, where surf-pounded rocks are home to sea anemones, sea stars, and barnacle colonies.

SECOND BEACH
Our rating: Easy (but stairs and boardwalk may be very slippery)
Distance: 5.75 km (return)
Time: 2 hours + (return, including beach walk and play)
Elevation loss: 100 m (all elevation loss is at the last section, where stairs descend to the beach)

Drive from Rialto Beach to the intersection of La Push and Mora roads; turn right onto La Push Road. Just before the village of La Push, there is an unpaved parking area on the left and easy-to-see signage for Second Beach.

A wide, dirt trail dips down to a spring on the left (a water source for the Quillayute fish hatchery), then gently ascends into lush, rich rainforest, with enormous stumps and hollowed-out tree trunks bordering the trail (great fun for little ones). These are the vestiges of logging, which took place before the area was protected. The trail meanders gently and is cool and shady, with light filtering through the canopy far above.

Closer to the ocean, the sound of surf rises and the sky beyond the fringe of ancient trees opens up. A long boardwalk staircase switches back and forth, dropping from the forest's edge down to the beach.

The fine-sand beach is often shrouded in mist, but be patient and with luck you will see the haunting forms of the sea stacks emerge from the clouds, just offshore. The tallest stack is known as Crying Lady Rock. Beyond are the Quillayute Needles—a grouping of both pointy and flat-topped rocks. Heading south along the beach, you can walk as far as Teahwhit Head, crossing several small creeks. There are numerous rock clusters to explore, home to intertidal life including starfish and anemones.

What you might see

The Pacific here is home to sea otters and Steller's sea lions. Watch for black oystercatchers screeching above the surf. Bald eagles are not uncommon, and there is abundant intertidal life.

What to bring

- I.D. for crossing the U.S./Canada border. Check with the M.V. *Coho* ferry staff or the U.S. Consulate in Vancouver for current requirements.
- Hard-sided, snap-top food containers. Available at Mora Ranger Station.
- Maps. Washington State Highway map (available at BCAA or bookstores) and an Olympic National Park map (write for this ahead of time, or pick one up at a ranger station).
- Rubber boots. Very useful for beach camping. Easy to pull on and off when getting in and out of the tent. The footwear of choice for little people who like to splash in any available water.
- Tide tables. You can get these online at http://www.windsox.us/VISITOR/weather.html. Click on "Tide Charts—Washington State" and view the tables for La Push. You can print these out at home, and arrive prepared. Or you can purchase a tide table at Mora Ranger Station.

- Star chart. On a clear night, the night sky is incredible. Small fold-out laminated star charts are available at many bookstores.

Bad-weather planning

One summer we had just spent two glorious days in the Elwha, and on a sunny, hot morning in mid-July, we drove to Rialto Beach for a change of scenery. Ten minutes from the turnoff, we noted a huge, dark-grey cloud hanging low on the horizon, where the forest meets the ocean, as far as the eye could see. The Rialto Beach parking lot was shrouded in wet fog, and we could barely see 10 m ahead. The beach was socked in the whole time we were there. This area has its own unique weather: be prepared. This is one destination where a backup plan to deal with wet weather is not just advisable, but absolutely essential—this area is one of the wettest in the U.S., and the coast has its own weather system. Don't be fooled by blue skies inland; the coast is more often than not cloaked in fog and drizzle.

Even when there's rain like you've never seen before, you may not want to turn around and immediately head for the Port Angeles ferry lineup. Here are some options.

DRY OUT GEAR

There are laundromats at the Three Rivers Resort (junction of Mora and La Push roads), or in Forks.

DITCH THE TENT

Motels can get very appealing in soggy weather. Expect to pay on average US $80 per night for a motel. Before you leave home, pick up a Washington accommodation guide from BCAA if you're a member, or go to the Forks Chamber of Commerce website (www.forkswa.com) and print out the accommodation listings to bring along.

Low-budget options that we haven't personally tried include: Rainforest Hostel, Tel: 360-374-2270, south of Forks near Ruby Beach, family room available; and Hoh Humm Ranch Bed and Breakfast, Tel: 360-374-5337, 32 km south of Forks, 10 km from Ruby Beach.

HEAD INDOORS

Forks Public Library. Find the children's section and curl up to read some stories. The library is located on the main street.

Forks Timber Museum. You'll find a pioneer kitchen, farm equipment, vintage newspapers and photographs, logging equipment, and a fire-lookout tower. Admission is by donation.

Makah Museum in Neah Bay. Make this a day trip. Drive 70 km from Forks north to Neah Bay to visit this fine tribal museum with full-sized replica longhouse, cedar dugout canoes, whaling, sealing, and fishing gear, basketry, and other tools.

Hoh Rainforest Visitor Center. Drive 40 km southeast of Forks to the only temperate coniferous rainforest in the world. The Hall of Mosses walk is an easy self-guided interpretative walk through a living cathedral of luminous green (30 – 40 minutes, return trip). It would only add to the moodiness of the place to do this walk in the rain! There is a park visitor centre that has exhibits and washrooms.

Campfire

It's growing dark and getting cooler. We pull on our fleece jackets as we clean up after our meal. The tin cooking pot is coated with a thin layer of grease. I scrub it gently and walk away from the campsite to carefully empty the dishwater. Joseph boils water for hot chocolate. Elena is happily collecting twigs of driftwood. Under her sweater and red rubber boots, she is wearing a fuzzy baby-blue sleeper with feet.

I crumple bits of used paper, and Elena and I build a teepee with her driftwood sticks. Then we all watch, transfixed, as Joseph strikes a match and holds it to the paper, where a flame leaps into life. We all discuss how best to build the fire, where to place the next piece of wood, whether we need to fan it to give it more air. When we are satisfied with our engineering, we balance on driftwood benches. The hot chocolate is ready, the sky is dark indigo, the outlines of the beach barely visible. The water looks black. We aren't tired. The night air is still and we are wide, wide awake. Sometimes we take a stick and poke it in the glowing embers under the collapsing teepee.

We tell stories and wonder about the constellations. We sit in the dark and peaceful night forever, until the fire is a bed of coals. There is a hiss as Joseph pours water over it, then Elena scoops sand and covers the still steaming coals. We push the stones into a tight ring around the fire bed and make sure it is safe to leave it.

Smelling of smoke, we unzip the tent door and leave our shoes under the fly. We are full of our campfire, our tales, and the night sky. Within moments, we are asleep.

RESOURCES

Checklist 1: The Ten Essentials

HAVE	NEED	ITEM	PACKED
		Water (at least one litre per person) for a day hike, plus water purification system for overnight trips (or stove/pot/fuel)	
		Emergency food supply for ___ persons	
		Raingear and warm clothing for each family member	
		First-aid kit	
		Army knife or multi-purpose tool	
		Map	
		Compass	
		Firestarter and matches	
		Flashlight and extra bulbs and batteries	
		Large orange plastic bag for each family member	

NOTE: These lists are designed for two stages of preparation: first, for checking to see if you actually have the items on hand (or whether you need to find, borrow or buy them) and second, for ensuring all the items are packed for the trip.

Other emergency items

HAVE	NEED	ITEM	PACKED
		Five metres of nylon cord or webbing	
		Wire or duct tape	
		Signal mirror	
		Cash for telephone	
		Single-edge razor blades	
		Plastic tarp for emergency shelter	
		Lightweight space blanket	

Checklist 2: Day pack, adult

HAVE	NEED	ITEM	PACKED
		Water (at least one litre per person) for a day hike	
		Trail food	
		Emergency energy bars supply for each person in group	
		Map and compass	
		First-aid kit	
		Wet wipes	
		Sanitary products	
		Allergy medication	
		Extra personal prescription medicine	
		Army knife or multi-purpose tool	
		Fire starter and matches in waterproof container	
		Small flashlight and extra bulbs and batteries	
		Large orange plastic bag for each person in group (can be used to hold other items and ensure they are kept dry, in emergencies for keeping people dry, or for signalling for help)	
		Polyethylene sheet (2 m x 2 m) plus cord for emergency shelter	
		Whistle for each person in group	
		Bear bells	
		Zip-lock bag of toilet paper (if you remove the cardboard roll on a half-finished roll, the remaining half-roll is very compact).	
		Plastic trowel in plastic bag (for digging latrine holes)	
		Empty zip-lock bag for packing out toilet paper	
		Raingear for each family member	
		Insulated top and bottom for each family member	
		Warm hat and gloves for each family member	
		Sunhats for each family member	
		Extra pair of socks for each family member	
		Car keys (one set for each adult)	

Optional extras
- This book! (or other trail-guide book)
- Plant or intertidal life identification book
- Telescopic hiking poles
- Camera and extra film
- Binoculars
- Writing and drawing supplies

Checklist 3: Day pack, child

HAVE	NEED	ITEM	PACKED
		Water bottle	
		Trail snacks	
		Emergency energy bar	
		Bandana	
		Whistle	
		Large orange plastic bag	
		Kid's Kit items (lightstick, space blanket, signal mirror, personal care items) See "Safety" chapter for info on assembling a Kid's Kit	
		Sunhat (if parents are not carrying it)	
		Raingear (if parents are not carrying it)	
		Warm pants (if parents are not carrying them)	
		Warm hat and gloves (if parents are not carrying them)	

Optional extras
- Science kit: plastic bug jar with a lid, magnifying glass
- Writing and drawing supplies

Keep a checklist in your day packs

We keep our first-aid supplies prepacked and ready to go in one of our day packs. We also keep a copy of our day-pack-contents checklist in a pocket of the pack.

If we decide on the spur of the moment to head out for an afternoon hike, we can quickly go through our checklists. That way, we aren't tempted to cut corners and not bother to bring things because we are pressed for time.

Checklist 4: Overnight gear

HAVE	NEED	ITEM	PACKED
		PACKS	
		Overnight backpack(s)	
		Child carrier pack	
		Day pack (and children's day packs)	
		Fanny pack	
		Stuff sacks for clothing x _____	
		Compression stuff sacks for sleeping bags x _____	
		SHELTER	
		Tent	
		Tent poles	
		Tent fly	
		Tent stakes and lines	
		Groundsheet (if needed)	
		Tarp, tarp poles, tarp ropes	
		Sleeping bags x _____ people	
		Sleeping pads x _____ people	
		Small flashlight to suspend in tent	
		COOKING	
		Backpacking stove and its windscreen	
		Leak-proof fuel bottle (full)	
		Extra fuel	
		Lighter and/or matches (in waterproof bag)	
		Cooking pots and pot grips	
		Lightweight frying pan	
		Insulated cups x _____ people	
		Lightweight bowls x _____ people	
		Spoons x _____	
		Forks x _____	
		Baby spoon and plastic baby bowl with snap lid	
		Folding can opener (if you are bringing canned food)	
		Tiny nylon cutting board	
		Large spoon	
		Kitchen knife	
		Biodegradable soap	
		Dish scrubber	

continued on next page

Checklist 4: Overnight gear (continued)

HAVE	NEED	ITEM	PACKED
		Lightweight, quick-drying dish towel	
		Zip-lock bags for garbage	
		Lightweight tablecloth (if desired)	
		FOOD (SEE MENUS)	
		Spice kit	
		Day 1: breakfast, lunch, supper	
		Day 2: breakfast, lunch, supper	
		Day 3: breakfast, lunch, supper	
		Collapsible water bag	
		Water	
		Water purification system	
		Emergency food	
		Trail snacks	
		TOILETRIES	
		Contact-lens solution	
		Hairbrush and/or comb	
		Hair elastics or barrettes	
		Toothbrushes x _____ people	
		Biodegradable toothpaste	
		Biodegradable soap	
		Wash cloth	
		Lightweight, quick-drying towel	
		Trowel wrapped in plastic bag	
		Zip-lock bag, with toilet paper roll x 2	
		Zip-lock bags (empty) for dirty toilet paper x 2	
		Zip-lock bag of wet wipes x 2	
		Sanitary items	
		Disposable and/or cloth diapers	
		Diaper cream	
		SAFETY ESSENTIALS	
		Fully stocked first-aid kit (see separate checklist)	
		Map in a zip-lock bag	
		Compass	
		Firestarter and matches	
		Flashlight and extra bulbs and batteries	

Checklist 4: Overnight gear (continued)

HAVE	NEED	ITEM	PACKED
		Large orange plastic bag for each person in group	
		5 m of nylon cord or webbing	
		Wire and duct tape	
		Signal mirror	
		Cash for telephone	
		Plastic tarp for emergency shelter	
		Lightweight space blanket	
		PERSONAL ESSENTIALS	
		Extra prescription medicine (in case you are held up)	
		Allergy medication	
		Zip-lock bag "wallet" with personal I.D., cash, permits, health card, insurance etc.	
		Car keys (each adult should have a set)	
		Prescription glasses	
		Sunglasses	
		OPTIONAL	
		Telescopic hiking pole(s) or ski poles	
		Camera	
		Film	
		Binoculars	
		Journal or sketchbook	
		Pen/pencil	
		FUN (CUSTOMIZE THIS LIST FOR YOUR FAMILY)	
		Hacky sack or ball	
		Length(s) of thick rope	
		Frisbee	
		Star guide	
		Magnifying glass	
		Aquarium net(s)	
		Paper and pencils	
		Deck of cards	

Checklist 5: Infant clothing

HAVE	NEED	ITEM	PACKED
		Diapers	
		Diaper covers	
		Change cloth	
		Diaper rash lotion	
		Garbage bag for used diapers	
		Hat for cold weather	
		Hat for sun protection	
		Polyester socks	
		Extra socks	
		Mittens (or socks as substitute)	
		Bib	
		Undershirts	
		Sleeper suit(s)	
		Fleece sweater or jacket	
		Rainsuit—or poncho-style rainwear to go over infant in child carrier	
		Windbreaker	
		Shoes	

Checklist 6: Adult clothing

HAVE	NEED	ITEM	PACKED
		Underwear	
		Long underwear top (or other insulating top)	
		Long underwear (or other insulating bottom)	
		Sleepwear	
		T-shirt (long-sleeved or short-sleeved)*	
		Fleece or lightweight wool pullover	
		Lightweight long pants or leggings (not cotton)*	
		Pile jacket or wool sweater	
		Windbreaker with hood	
		Rainjacket	
		Rainpants	
		Quick-dry shorts	
		Swimsuit	
		Toque/hat for cold weather and evenings	
		Hat for sun protection	
		Mittens or gloves (always!)	
		Fast-dry socks	
		Wool socks	
		Hiking boots (dry shoes)	
		Sports sandals (wet shoes)	
		Extra shoelaces	
		Camp shoes (flip-flops work well)	
		Rubber boots (if suitable to destination)	
		Sunglasses	

*For multi-day trips, bring more than one.

Checklist 7: Child clothing

HAVE	NEED	ITEM	PACKED
		Underwear x ___ days	
		Long underwear top (or other insulating top)	
		Long underwear (or other insulating bottom)	
		Sleepwear	
		T-shirt (long-sleeved), preferably synthetic*	
		T-shirt (short-sleeved)*	
		Fleece or lightweight wool pullover	
		Lightweight long pants or leggings (not cotton)*	
		Pile jacket or wool sweater	
		Windbreaker with hood	
		Rainjacket	
		Rainpants	
		Quick-dry shorts	
		Swimsuit	
		Toque/hat for cold weather & evenings	
		Hat for sun protection	
		Mittens or gloves (always!)	
		Fast-dry socks	
		Wool socks	
		Hiking boots or high-top runners (dry shoes)	
		Sports sandals (wet shoes)	
		Camp shoes (flip-flops work well)	
		Rubber boots (if suitable to destination)	
		Sunglasses	

*For multi-day trips, bring more than one.

Checklist 8: First-aid kit

HAVE	NEED	ITEM	PACKED
		MEDICINES AND DRUGS	
		Adult pain relief tablets for muscle ache or inflammation (Aspirin or ibuprofen)	
		Adult pain and fever reduction tablets (acetaminophen)	
		Children's pain and fever reduction medicine (acetaminophen)	
		Adult antihistamine	
		Children's antihistamine	
		Allergy medicine—or Epi-Pen (injectible epinephrine)	
		Diarrhea medicine	
		Antacid tablets	
		Motion sickness tablets	
		Ipecac syrup (for poison) CAUTION: Not to be confused with Ipepac, which is anti-nausea medicine	
		Throat lozenges	
		Gatorade crystals	
		SKIN CARE	
		SPF sunscreen 30+	
		Medicated lip balm	
		Aloe vera (for burns)	
		Rash or skin-irritation lotion (e.g. Calamine)	
		Blister pads (e.g. Moleskin)	
		Insect repellent	
		Anti-sting lotion	
		ANTISEPTIC & ANTIBIOTIC	
		Antiseptic solution (to cleanse skin around wound)	
		Sterile wipes	
		Antibiotic ointment (to prevent infection in minor cuts)	
		BANDAGING MATERIALS	
		Band-aids	
		Children's novelty bandages (these can work wonders!)	
		Butterfly bandages	
		Triangular bandage (for holding dressings in place)	
		Sanitary napkins (for use as pressure bandages)	
		Sterile dressings (7 x 7 cm)	
		Sterile gauze pads (5 x 5 cm, or 10 x 10 cm)	
		Non-sticky dressing like Telfa pads	

continued on next page

Checklist 8: First-aid kit (continued)

HAVE	NEED	ITEM	PACKED
		Bandage tape	
		Gauze rolls (5 cm; 10 cm)	
		Elastic wrap (8 cm)	
		Waterproof barrier to put over bandages (could be waterproof tape or a condom)	
		EQUIPMENT	
		Thermometer (and plastic cover)	
		Tweezers	
		Scissors	
		Safety pins	
		Q-tips (for cleaning wounds)	
		Cotton balls	
		Needle and thread	
		First-aid instruction booklet	

Checklist 9: Are you ready to go?

	VEHICLE
	Checked oil and packed spare oil and coolant
	Checked washer fluid
	Checked fuel
	Checked tire pressure
	Checked spare tire
	Exterior loads secure
	Road map and directions in car
	All gear in car
	PACKED FOR EASY ACCESS IN THE CAR
	Diaper bag
	Wet wipes or wet cloth in plastic bag
	Small tea towel for wipe-ups
	Nutritious snacks
	Water bottles
	Mints or ginger snaps for car sickness
	Zip-lock bags for car sickness
	Bag for garbage
	Pillows
	Blankets
	Window sun shades
	Toys, activities for each child
	Children's music and/or book tapes
	WALLET, ID, PERMITS
	Cash
	Credit card(s)
	Family ID
	Driver's licences
	Permits and maps
	Guidebooks
	Trip plan has been left with friend

	LEAVING THE HOUSE
	Check thermostat
	Automatic timers on
	Stove and oven off
	Toaster, coffee pot, etc. unplugged
	Windows closed and locked
	Garbages out
	Everyone has gone to the bathroom
	Toilets flushed
	Front, rear, and side doors locked
	Have taken extra car keys

FIRST-AID GUIDELINES

Shock
SYMPTOMS
- Weakness
- Pale colour
- Cool, clammy skin
- Irregular breathing
- Nausea
- Dizziness
- Shivering

TREATMENT
- Keep the person at a comfortable temperature, so that they don't become overheated or hypothermic
- If the person is cold, wrap in emergency blanket, sleeping bag, jacket
- If the person is warm, create shade
- Keep the person lying down and comfortable
- If there is a head injury, don't raise feet

Blisters
PREVENTION
- Wear two pairs of socks (a thin liner plus a thicker cushion of wool or wool blend)
- Keep boots clear of debris inside
- Don't hike for long periods with wet feet
- If you feel discomfort, stop immediately

TREATMENT
- If only redness or discomfort (a "hot spot"), apply blister pad or tape to the spot to coat friction area and protect from further rubbing
- If blister is starting, cut doughnut of foam and surround blister
- If blister is broken, clean with soap and water, put on a dressing and blister pad

Blister pads will not stick properly to sweaty or dirty feet; clean the area so it will stick well.

Do not open blisters unless they are larger than a nickel. If you must open it, wash hands and skin with soap. Sterilize needle over a flame (hold end with a cloth); let it cool. Pierce the edge of the blister (not the centre). Gently massage until all fluid drains. Apply antibiotic ointment and a light bandage. Check for signs of infection.

Burns

TREATMENT

If you are dealing with a minor burn:
- Plunge burned area into cool water to reduce pain
- Clean with soap and water
- If needed, apply topical anesthetic for pain

If you are dealing with a serious burn, get immediate medical attention.

Sunburn

PREVENTION
- Use SPF 30+ and apply to all exposed areas
- Wear wide-brimmed hat
- Wear sunglasses

TREATMENT
- Cover burn with loose clothing
- Apply aloe vera for soothing
- Keep clean (do not break blisters if they form)

Cuts

TREATMENT

Clean with antibacterial soap and water. Draw edges of wound together, then apply pressure. Elevate wound. If bleeding persists, tape edges of wound with butterfly bandage, then:
- Apply clean, non-sticking dressing
- Secure it with adhesive tape
- If significant bleeding, apply pressure to wound with sterile compress
- Elevate wound above level of heart to slow bleeding
- Continue replacing dressings and applying pressure until bleeding stops
- When bleeding stops, wrap with a compression bandage and go for help
- If bleeding does not stop, evacuate immediately

Eyes

(chemical or other contaminant)

TREATMENT
- Flush generously with water, using a gentle, continuous stream of water
- Flush from near bridge of nose, outwards (so you won't send the contaminant into the opposite eye)
- Continue flushing with water 10 – 15 minutes, until certain everything has been removed
- Cover injured eye with sterile gauze pad
- Go to hospital

Heat Exhaustion

- Eat well
- Drink two to four litres of water per day (everyone have a big drink before setting off)
- Wear sunglasses and light-coloured clothing
- Wear a hat with a wide brim
- Rest in shade
- Reduce activity during very hot weather

SYMPTOMS

- Dizziness
- Pale skin
- Restlessness
- Nausea
- Rapid heartbeat
- Headache

TREATMENT

- Remove heat source (take off clothing, get into shade, etc.)
- Sponge down to cool person off
- Give sips of liquid fortified with electrolyte supplement (like Gatorade) or with salt

Heat Stroke

PREVENTION

Same as for heat exhaustion.

SYMPTOMS

- Sudden onset
- Confusion, irrational behaviour
- Rapid pulse
- Hot, dry skin
- Unconsciousness

TREATMENT

- Remove heat source
- Moisten body with cool water
- Fan to increase circulation and cooling (don't cool excessively to a hypothermic state)
- Evacuate to hospital

Hypothermia

Hypothermia is the number-one killer in the outdoors. It can occur quickly from being wet and cold, or slowly from long exposure to cold, wind, and rain. You can get hypothermia even when it is as warm as 10°C.

- Eat high-energy, high-protein foods regularly
- Drink adequate fluids
- Replace electrolytes (eat bananas, tomatoes)
- Dress properly for the weather
- Keep body and clothing dry (from sweat and outside moisture) and protected from wind
- Cover head, neck, and hands (most body heat is lost through the head)
- Don't wear cotton; wear clothes with insulating properties, even when wet (synthetics like polypropylene or natural fibres like wool)

SYMPTOMS (*=SEVERE SYMPTOM)
- Feeling cold and shivering
- Difficulty performing simple physical movements
- Apathy
- Slurred speech*
- Unresponsiveness*
- Mental confusion*

TREATMENT
- Stop hiking
- Remove damp clothing (or add warm insulation)
- Build a fire or heat water
- Give warm liquids and high-energy food if the person is able to take them, but avoid tea, coffee, and alcohol because they cause loss of body fluid
- If you can't get to a hospital quickly, apply warmth to the body. Focus on head, neck, armpits, and groin because the body core will get heat from these. Use warm blankets or another person's body.

Insect Bites and Stings
PREVENTION
- Wear long-sleeved tops and long pants
- Make sure campsites are well away from swampy or low-lying areas

TREATMENT
- Remove stingers by scraping with a knife edge or fingernail
- Don't use tweezers or pull stingers—this can squeeze more venom into wound
- Wash with soap and water
- Apply anti-sting lotion or a paste of baking powder and water

FOR ALLERGIC REACTION
- Give antihistamine
- Keep person calm
- Evacuate to hospital

RECIPES

If you're stuck on what to cook for a main meal, here are a few of our personal favourites to get you started—trail tested and recommended by us and our children! There are loads of excellent backcountry cookbooks available, with recipes to suit every palate. When packing and preparing your ingredients at home, don't forget to include the cooking directions with each meal package.

One-pot backpack recipes

These one-pot meals use lightweight, compact ingredients that you prep ahead of time at home so they are packed for maximum efficiency and minimum bulkiness—essential if you are hiking in a good distance to your tent site. With only adults able to carry supplies, the lighter you pack, the easier your trip will be. All dry ingredients go into a single bag, using the corners of the bag to tie off seasonings and extras separately from the other ingredients.

The following one-pot recipes are favourites of ours adapted from *Backcountry Cooking: From Pack to Plate in 10 Minutes* by Dorcas Miller, ©1998. Reprinted/adapted with permission of the publisher, The Mountaineers, Seattle, WA. This book is an excellent resource and is available from the Victoria public library.

PENNE WITH MUSHROOMS AND SHRIMP

Ingredients are for one adult serving. Multiply as necessary.

At home, combine in plastic bag and tie off:
- 1 tbsp powdered butter
- ¼ cup Parmesan cheese
- ¼ tsp garlic powder
In another corner, tie off:
- ¼ cup dried mushrooms, cut into large slices
In remainder of bag, place:
- ¾ cup penne
Pack one can of water-packed shrimp.

On trail. Boil 3 – 4 cups water. Add penne. Stir so pasta doesn't stick to pot. Add mushrooms about 5 minutes before pasta is done. When pasta is *al dente,* pour off all liquid, except ½ cup. Stir in dry seasoning ingredients to make a light sauce. Add salt and pepper to taste. Stir in shrimp.

INTERNATIONAL COUSCOUS

Ingredients are for one adult serving. Multiply as necessary.

At home, place in plastic bag and tie off in a corner:
- 1½ tbsp toasted sliced almonds
To the rest of the bag, add:
- ¼ cup + 2 tbsp couscous
- 2 tsp dried cranberries
- 2 tsp currants or raisins
- 2 tsp thinly sliced dried carrots
- 2 tsp dried onions
- 1½ tsp chicken bouillon powder

- 1½ tsp chili powder
- ½ tsp garlic powder
- ¼ tsp brown sugar

On trail. Put all ingredients except almonds in insulated bowl (or you can use a cooking pot, wrapped with an insulating sweater or blanket). Add ½ cup + 1½ tbsp boiling water. Mix well, cover, let stand 10 minutes. Add almonds.

MASHED POTATO DINNER

Ingredients are for one adult serving. Multiply as necessary.

At home, pack (in separate bags):
- 1½ cups instant mashed potatoes
- 1 tbsp butter
- 3 – 4 scallions or a few green onions
- 1 small carrot
- 1 oz (1-inch cube) cheddar cheese
- 1½- inch pepperoni stick (about 1 oz)

On trail. Add 1½ cups boiling water to the instant mashed potatoes. Let stand 10 minutes. Slice fresh vegetables, cheese, and pepperoni. Fold into mashed potatoes along with the butter.

SCRAMBLED SUSHI DINNER

Ingredients are for one serving. Multiply as necessary.

At home, combine:
- ¾ cup instant rice
- 2 sheets nori (dried seaweed), broken into small pieces

- 1 square commercially dried tofu or several slices home-dried tofu (or bring fresh, pre-drained extra-firm tofu)
- 1 small carrot or ¼ cup thinly sliced dried carrots
Pack soy sauce.

On trail. Slice carrots. Place ingredients in insulated bowl and add 2 cups boiling water (2½ cups, if using dried carrots). Stir, cover, let stand 10 minutes (or until tofu has rehydrated). Season with soy sauce.

THAI SHRIMP WRAPS

Ingredients are for four cups of filling, enough for eight wraps.

At home, combine:
- 1 cup instant rice
- 2 tbsp + 2 tsp dried onion
- 2 tbsp + 2 tsp coconut cream powder or powdered coconut
- 2 tbsp + 2 tsp cilantro
- 2 tsp minced dried ginger
Pack separately:
- 1 (5 – 8 oz) can shrimp
- 8 soft tortillas

On trail. Place dry ingredients in insulated bowl, and add 1½ cups boiling water. Mix well, cover, let stand 10 min. Add drained shrimp to filling and roll.

BANANA BOATS

Ingredients make one banana boat. Adjust ingredients as necessary.

At home, pack:
- 1 banana (not too ripe)
- 3 to 4 marshmallows
- 2 squares of chocolate
- Tin foil

On trail. Make a lengthwise slit in banana. Insert marshmallows and chocolate into slit. Wrap in tin foil and bake over stove or in fire for 5-10 minutes. Take off fire and open tin foil. Eat with spoon.

COCONUT BALLS

Makes 10 balls.

At home, pack:
- Handful of cranberries
- ¼ cup instant cocoa or hot chocolate powder
- 2 cups desiccated coconut
- 1 small can of sweetened condensed milk, poured into a resealable container

On trail. Mix ingredients in bowl or pot. Form into balls. Serve.

PEARS HELEN

Serves up to five people, depending on number of pears used. Note: This recipe requires two pots.

At home. Pour 1 can sweetened condensed milk into a sealed container. Measure 2 oz Amaretto or other liqueur into a sealed container. Then pack:
- 1 – 2 dried pears per person
- 1 small Toblerone bar

On trail. Soak pears in water for half an hour. Fry pears in frying pan (with no oil) about 5 minutes, until hot. In separate pan, melt sweetened condensed milk and chocolate. Pour liqueur over pears and light liqueur with a match to flambé. Douse flames with chocolate mixture and serve. The liqueur burns off in the fire.

FRUIT COBBLER

At home. Mix up your favourite cobbler topping at home, and put in a ziplock bag. Bring along fresh fruit.

On trail. Place fruit in pot. Add a small amount of water to keep fruit from burning and sticking to the pot bottom. Put cobbler mixture on top of fruit. Heat until fruit mixture is bubbling.

PLAY AND LEARNING ACTIVITIES

Gear and toys

Ball. Something easy to carry, large enough to kick or catch, and a bright colour so it is easy to find. Inflatable beach balls and hacky sacks work well.

Books. Tiny paperback books are perfect for keeping at-home bedtime routines. The Annikins series (just over one dollar per book) are good stories for under-sixes, and they are only 7.5 x 7.5 cm and weigh next to nothing.

Bug observation container. At home, make five or six air holes in a small, transparent, plastic food container. Look for insects under logs, rocks or leaves. Make sure you set your insect free after no more than one hour.

Child's compass. Practise taking sightings or finding your way in a meadow or on a beach.

Frisbee. This is also handy as a seat or a tray for carrying food!

Hiking journal. Bring along a mini-notebook (or make your own at home ahead of time).

Jacks. A tiny ball and a set of jacks take up very little space and are light, but can provide lots of entertainment.

Length of rope. An excellent prop for all kinds of adventures. Just give it to your children and see what they come up with! Make sure the rope is thick—string-width rope can be dangerous.

Lightweight kite on a short string. These can be very compact, and are good fun where there is a wide-open space, like a beach or a meadow.

Magnifying glass. For up-close examination of almost anything! (Also useful in case of emergency, to signal for help by flashing in the sun, or to start a fire. Make sure children understand they must not signal or start fires as a play activity.)

Mini-flashlights. You can get mini LED flashlights that are wonderful for small children (and for adults). They are tiny, clip onto a jacket zipper, and cast an amazingly large circle of light.

Music makers. A kazoo, a harmonica, a container and a stick for a drum, a couple of sticks or camp spoons knocked against each other, and you have a little band.

Paper and pencils. We like to cut up small squares of good-one-side paper and have each child bring a stack of these sheets in a zip-lock bag with a couple of sharpened pencils. Compact, waterproof, and great for games and rubbings as well as drawing.

Pick-up sticks. Cheap and easily available at the dollar store. Hazardous for under-twos, but good fun for toddlers to preschoolers. We like to play this in the tent or on a blanket or sleeping mat outside.

Playing cards. For extra-light cards, get a set of miniature playing cards from the dollar store.

Shovel and pail. For collecting treasures or building sandcastles.

Small net. Aquarium nets work well, and provide lots of fun anywhere there is water.

Small play people or animals. A few small people or animals can provide hours of fun. We pick up a few now and then at garage sales so we don't have to bring along (and potentially lose) our favourites from home.

Ways to motivate little hikers

The Colour Game. One person names a colour to look for. Everyone looks for things that are that colour.

Collect! Together with your children, choose something they can collect while hiking (again, no living plants or creatures)—pine cones, small stones, or interesting dead leaves are great. The prospect of "maybe there's another one around that corner!" can work like a charm. While your child is happily searching, you can look, too, and "plant" some—"Look! I see one!"

Find it on the map. This requires a little work at home ahead of time. Make a map for your child, with things for him to look for while hiking. It can be fun to have check-boxes to tick off after passing each landmark. Variation: Have children draw their map as they go along, showing what they see along the way. It can slow walkers down, but keeps motivation high.

Hide and seek. One adult and one child run ahead and hide behind a rock or tree. "Boo!" They jump out when the rest of the family approaches. Take turns all the way down the trail.

Hot sand. Ask everyone to imagine they are walking on different surfaces (hot sand, tacks, water, mud, wet grass, deep water, peanut butter, whipped cream, slick ice, sharp rocks, snow, etc.)

Leprechaun, where are you? Sachiko's family made up this game while trying to coax then-four-year-old Elena along the trail. We imagined that leprechauns were living in the plants that bordered the trail, and we looked for them! Some of the leprechauns wanted to hitch a ride on Elena's knapsack, others showed her their neat homes in the crooks of trees, others tried to make trouble, but we outsmarted them. The game completely absorbed her, and we made it all the way to our destination in record time. Kari's family has played a similar game, only they look for fairies living under toadstools.

Mystery bag. Pull out a stuff sack or empty plastic bag and collect items as you walk along the trail (acorns, pine cones, small stones, trash, etc., but no living plants or creatures). Once in a while, call out a stop for a peek in the mystery bag! Children put their hands

Christmas Trees for Squirrels

In *The Sense of Wonder,* Rachel Carson tells of the game she played with her grandson, Roger.

"There is a fine crop of young spruces coming along and one can find seedlings of almost any size down to the length of Roger's finger. I began to point out the baby trees.

'This one must be a Christmas tree for the squirrels,' I would say. 'It's just the right height. On Christmas Eve the red squirrels come and hang little shells and cones and silver threads of lichen on it for ornaments, and then the snow falls and covers it with shining stars, and in the morning the squirrels have a beautiful Christmas tree ... And this one is even tinier—it must be for little bugs of some kind—and maybe this bigger one is for the rabbits or woodchucks.'

Once this game was started it had to be played on all woods walks, which from now on were punctuated by shouts of, 'Don't step on the Christmas tree!' "

---

in the bag and try to guess what they are touching.

Name It! Everyone makes up their own names for features you pass along your hike—e.g., Mudpie Lake, Bubbly Creek, Mount Nose-So-High.

Sled Dog. If your child is losing motivation or is just meandering too slowly for the pace you would prefer, try pulling him with a walking stick (or ropes). Author Alice Cary (*Parents Guide to Hiking and Camping*) reports that one father adapts this method by using two sticks and pretending to be a sled dog. His boys love to yell at him as he barks and plays up his temporary persona.

Trail Tracks. One adult runs ahead and, using material found on the side of the trail, makes tracks for children to find and follow. Once the adult sets a few tracks, they can sit back and relax until the rest of the family catches up. Track suggestions: arrows made of twigs, a mound of acorns, pine cones, a leaf planted upright in the trail.

Treasure Hunter. This game works best when camp is near. Tell children a story of pirates or sailors burying treasure long ago at the very place camp will be. Once the family reaches camp, hide a treasure for kids to find—a bit of food, or "magic" shells and "power" rocks work well for our children.

See the "Chants and Songs" section for more ideas.

Nature appreciation activities

Bio-Diversity Circle. Make a circle on the ground with string or rope. Have children count how many living things they can find within the circle—soil counts!

Hug a Tree. Blindfold a child and lead them to a tree. Touch, smell, listen. Ask the child to describe the tree: its size, age, and shape. Once the child thinks he really knows the tree, lead him away, spin him around, and remove blindfold. Ask him to find the tree.

Listen to Your Senses. Blindfold two or more people. Have them sit quietly for a set amount of time. Then share what they heard, smelled, and felt.

Sames and Differences. The child looks at an object of their choice (a leaf, a rock, a flower). Ask them to look for another object that is similar in some way. In what ways is it the same? How is it different? Consider shape, texture, size, colour, and movement.

Scavenger Hunt. Collect only things that you can return safely, without damaging them. Make up your list based on the setting you are in. For example, find something that is:

- Round
- Fuzzy
- Sharp
- Perfectly straight
- Beautiful
- White
- Makes a noise
- Reminds you of yourself

Make up your own list of items. Two or more children could look for them in a radius around your camp (make sure they know the limits). Or you could all make a list together and then and go for a family walk to look for them. (Adapted from *Sharing Nature With Children* by Joseph Cornell)

Silent Sharing Walk. Walk in silence. When you spot something that catches your attention, tap the shoulder of the other people and point it out to them. "When a person becomes harmoniously attuned with the world, his feelings of harmony with other people are intensified, too. Through watching nature in silence, we discover within ourselves feelings of relatedness with whatever we see—plants, animals, stones, earth and sky." (Adapted from *Sharing Nature With Children* by Joseph Cornell)

Sun Clock

Find a straight stick. Push it into the ground or sand in an open, sunny place.

Every hour, place a rock where the stick's shadow stops. After you have marked out the hours, you should have a straight line of rocks on either side of the stick. At noon, there should be no shadow (the sun is straight overhead). One side of the stick will be shaded in the morning, the other in the afternoon.

Trust Walk. Let your child blindfold you and lead you around. Focus on sounds and textures. Then switch roles. Ask your children questions like: "What does the grass feel like?" "What can you hear?" "What can you smell?"

Other games and activities

Cooperative drawing. The first person draws a head and neck, then folds the paper so the head is hidden and only the neck shows. The next person adds on from the neck and draws the body to the waist (and the arms), then folds the paper so only the waist shows. Next—legs to the ankles. The last person does the feet. The last person gets to unfold it and see the weird creature you have drawn together!

Do This, Do That (variation of "Simon Says"). No one is supposed to move unless the leader says "Do this." The leader does an action, and says, "Do this". Everyone imitates the leader's action. If the leader does an action and says, "Do that," no one is supposed to move!

Hot or Cold. Beware—this can get very noisy! One person is "it". He leaves the group. The group chooses one object for her to touch. The person is called back. As she tries to guess the object, everyone else claps to show if she's getting close. The louder, the closer; the softer the clapping, the farther away.

Memory Game. Place a number of common objects on a table. Let people study them for about one minute. Cover everything with a cloth. Each person lists as many things as they can remember seeing. Remove the cloth. Players get one point for each thing remembered; minus two points for each thing missed. Variation: After everyone has studied the things, they must turn their backs. Move several objects to different places. Players have to list what has been moved.

Popcorn. Everyone squats, pretending they are corn kernels waiting to pop when they hear the number "10." Start counting 1, 2, 3, 4 ... When you reach 10, they go from the squat to jumping all around, until you start a new batch of popcorn.

Rock, Scissors, Paper. Each player puts one hand behind their back, and on the count of three, pulls it out in the shape of paper (palm open), rock (fist), or scissors (like a peace sign—two fingers open). Scoring: Paper covers rock; rock breaks scissors; scissors cut paper; scoring is active, as one player gently acts out the appropriate action on the other player.

Whispers. Whisper the name of a person in the group very, very softly. When the person hears his name, he jumps up and raises his hand (or substitute another action). This can be fun in the tent.

Who Am I? Act like an animal and see who can figure out what you are! Or impersonate someone you know.

Songs and chants

Animal Like Me Chant
Chant: "If I were an animal, I would be, Someone—just like me!"
Response:
"If I were an animal, I would be a ... because it's good at ... just like me!"
Example: "If I were an animal, I would be an otter, because it's good at playing just like me!" (from *Self Esteem Games,* by Barbara Sher).

Clap the Same
One person claps a simple beat and the others imitate the clap (or you could do this by humming a beat).

I've Got A Sound Inside of Me
Family says: "Elena has a sound inside of her that goes like ..."
Elena: "Yooooouuuup!"
Family: "Yooup, yooup, yooup!"
Family says: "Mama has a sound inside of her that goes like ..."
Mama: "Oooooooh!"
Family: "Oooh, oooh, oooh!"
(from *Self-Esteem Games* by Barbara Sher)

Going on a Bear Hunt
Adapt to your surroundings.
"I'm going on a bear hunt,
But I am not afraid!
Oh! MUD ...
Can't go over it,
Can't go around it,
Can't go under it,
Have to go through it!
Squelch, squelch, squelch."

Let's Walk in A Circle
Let's walk in a circle,
Let's walk in a circle
Let's walk in a circle,
Let's do it right now!

Let's walk way down low,
Let's walk way down low,
Let's walk way down low
Let's do it right now!
(Variations: On your heels, on your toes, really softly, sideways, backwards, like a robot, like a rag doll, like the Tin Man, etc.)

Rainstorm Song. Make a rainstorm. Start by rubbing hands together gently. Slowly rub harder, then start to clap. Clap louder and louder as the rainstorm grows stronger.

Campsite and tent games

Continuous Story. This can be hilarious! Sachiko still remembers the punchline of an infamous story told in the family tent when she was a girl. One person starts with the opening line of the story, but leaves the end of the sentence hanging for the next person to finish and carry on. For example:
Person 1: "Once upon a time there was a beautiful ..."
Person 2: "... little slug named Beatrice, who was ..."
Person 3: "... sliding along the wet grass just outside the ..."
and so on!

Spin the Bottle (or stick, or spoon, etc.)
Face each other and spin an object.
When it stops spinning, the "top" will
be pointing at someone. Whoever spun
the object says something positive
about the person it's pointing at (even
herself, if the spinner is pointing at her).
It could be a story, a good memory, a
quality you admire, etc. Use this phrase:
"When I see (name of person), what
makes me smile inside is …"
(from *Self-Esteem Games* by
Barbara Sher)

Fantasy Land. Ask each other thought-
provoking questions like: If people from
another planet landed on Earth and
wanted to see the most beautiful thing
on our planet, what would you show
them? If you could only eat one food
for the rest of your life, what would it
be? If you could be another person for
a day, who would you be? Why? If you
could go anywhere in the world, where
would you go? Why?

Hand Shadows. Our children can't wait
to get to bed so they can turn on their
flashlights and play hand shadows!

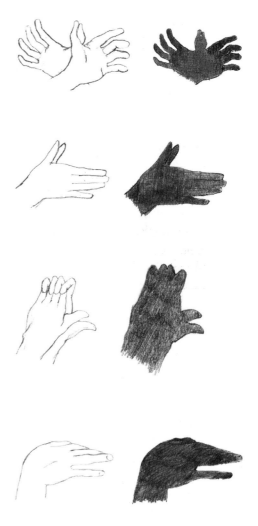

**Hand shadow shapes: (top to bottom) spider, dog,
rooster, and goose.**

IDENTIFICATION GUIDE

There is so much to see in the wild. This identification guide lists only a very few of the most common things you might find on your adventures to destinations in this book. If this whets your appetite for identifying nature's wonders, there are many excellent locally focussed guidebooks available. Some of our favourites are listed in the resources section at the back of the book.

Sea Mammals

GREY WHALE

- Annually migrate 12,000 miles from the Arctic to California and back
- Frequently "spy hop"—put their heads out of water and take a look around
- Have no teeth, but use baleen (long strips of whalebone that hang from the mouth) to filter food

Fun Fact
A baby grey whale drinks enough milk to fill more than 2,000 baby bottles a day.

ORCA (KILLER WHALE)

- The largest member of the dolphin family
- Resident orcas live off the B.C. coast, and transient orcas pass through
- Hunt all kinds of prey, including fish, squid, seabirds, seals, and even blue whales

Fun Fact
Orcas use clicking, whistles, and scream-like sounds to communicate. Each pod (family group) has its own "sound"—recognizable from several miles away.

PACIFIC WHITE-SIDED DOLPHIN

- Dark grey to black in colour, with white belly, throat, and chin
- Tall black-grey dorsal (back) fin
- Very acrobatic, love to bowride (ride in the bow-wave of boats) and leap
- Usually seen offshore in groups of over 50

Fun Fact
Dolphins use a technique called echolocation, which means they make clicking sounds to judge distances and find food.

DALL'S PORPOISE

- Have a triangular white-tipped dorsal (back) fin
- Often travel in groups of 10 – 20, but sometimes in groups of over 1,000

Fun Fact

When swimming fast, Dall's porpoises create a V-shaped splash called a "rooster tail."

HARBOUR PORPOISE

- Smallest cetacean (an order of fishlike sea mammals) found in B.C. waters
- Found in shallow, murky waters, like bays and estuaries
- Not as acrobatic as other cetaceans

RIVER OTTER

- Live in rivers and oceans
- Often mistaken for a sea otter, but are actually a member of the weasel family
- Distinguished from sea otters by their long tail, and because they like to come on shore

MINK

- Live along water banks
- Can dive up to five metres and are great swimmers
- Are nocturnal

Fun Fact

Minks kill by biting victims on the neck. They hunt rabbits, mice, chipmunks, fish, snakes, frogs, turtles and some birds.

STELLER'S SEA LION

- Named after a German naturalist, who called it "lion of the sea" because of its golden eyes and loud roar
- Largest rookeries are on islands off the northern tip of Vancouver Island, where there are between 4,000 and 5,000 sea lions

CALIFORNIA SEA LION

- Smaller and darker than Steller's
- Honk, whereas Steller's bark
- Females and juveniles stay south; only the males come to B.C. waters

Fun Fact

While learning to swim, California sea lion pups often rest on their mother's back.

PACIFIC HARBOUR SEAL

- Much smaller than sea lions
- Love to sunbathe on beaches and rocks

Fun Fact

Harbour seals can dive 400 m and stay under water for close to 30 minutes!

Intertidal Zone

ANEMONE

- Can move very slowly, but are usually attached to rocks or shells
- Flick sticky tentacles to capture food such as shrimp and crabs
- Tuck tentacles in if in danger or if in dry air

BARNACLE

- Are always attached to a smooth object
- Get food by using feet to kick plant and animals from the water into their mouth

CHITON

- Shell is made of eight overlapping plates
- Can roll up in a ball when disturbed
- Crawls on rocks using a kind of tongue to scrape off tiny plants

Fun Fact

Chitons are very ancient creatures; they have lived on earth for 500 million years.

CLAM

- Two hinged shells, so are called "bivalves"
- Live under the sand and send two long siphons to the surface for food and water (water spurts out as they retract the siphons)
- BEWARE of red tide, a potentially fatal disease that can live in clams. Do not harvest unless you are certain it is safe. No harvesting is allowed in national or provincial parks.

CRAB

- Many species, but all have four pairs of legs and a pair of pincers
- Sex can be identified by the abdominal flap—like a "V" in the male; wider and like a "U" in the female

Fun Fact

Crabs molt (lose their entire outer shells, including their eye coverings) many times during their life.

LIMPET

- Called "univalves" because they have only one shell
- Glide at night on their one foot, looking for food
- Have long tongues that scrape algae off rocks

MOON JELLY

- Made mostly of water—no heart, brain, or bones
- The four horseshoe shapes seen through the top of the translucent body are the reproductive organs
- Caution! Tentacles can cause a rash

Fun Fact

Moon jellies are bioluminescent, meaning they are able to give off light.

MUSSEL

- Bivalves—have two hinged shells
- Open shells to feed on plants and animals; close shells when the tide goes out to keep from drying out
- BEWARE of red tide in mussels. Never harvest unless you are certain it is safe and legal to do so.

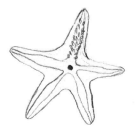

SEA STAR

- Can have between 5 and 40 arms
- Each arm has little tube feet on the underside for moving
- Eat by pushing the stomach through the mouth on the underside of the shell

Fun Fact

If a sea star loses an arm, it can grow another!

SEA URCHIN

- Use teeth in the mouth (underneath) for scraping and chewing food
- Can move slowly on little tube feet
- Caution! Spines can really hurt

Fun Fact

A sand dollar is in fact a type of sea urchin!

SEAWEED

- Don't have roots or leaves
- Use energy from the sun (photosynthesis) to grow

Fun Fact

Seaweed extracts are used in ice cream, chocolate milk, toothpaste, and paint!

SNAIL

- Are "gastropods"—"belly-footed animals"
- Have a hard foot that pokes out of their shells, which they use to move around

Fun Fact

Moon snails feed by drilling a hole in the shell of their prey and injecting an enzyme into the animal.

Amphibians

GARTER SNAKE

- Usually only 60 cm long
- Coloration varies; usually have dorsal strip of cream, yellow, orange, or red
- Eat slugs, earthworms, frogs, salamanders
- Not poisonous, but discharge a foul-smelling secretion if handled or frightened

PACIFIC TREE FROG

- Mating call of the male in the spring sounds like "wreck-it"
- Sticky pads on their feet help them climb and look for spiders and insects
- Leave the water in August or September and head for the trees

SALAMANDER AND NEWT

- Like to live under logs and rocks, where the air is moist
- Breathe through their skin

SLUG

- Member of the mollusc family, but have lost their shell
- Emit slime as a protective covering (if you get it on your hands, rub your hands together to remove it; don't wash—water makes it more sticky!)

Birds

BALD EAGLE

- Found only in North America
- Can fly up to 45 km per hour and dive at speeds up to 160 km per hour
- Keen eyesight—can spot fish at distances over a kilometre away

BLACK OYSTERCATCHER

- Able to open bivalves with their beak
- Sometimes quick enough to pick a mussel out of its shell before it can close

Fun Fact

Each oystercatcher inherits a particular shell-breaking technique from its parents.

BELTED KINGFISHER

- Easy to recognize in flight because of their large beaks and how they swoop over the water to catch fish

CORMORANT

- Sit on logs or rocks in the ocean, with beaks in the air and wings spread to dry
- In the sky, often fly in wedges like geese but are silent

Fun Fact

Cormorants are used in several countries as fishers. People place rings around the base of their necks so they cannot swallow the fish, but must give it up.

GREAT BLUE HERON

- Eat fish, frogs, salamanders, lizards, snakes, shrimps, crabs, crayfish, dragonflies, grasshoppers, and many aquatic insects
- Nest in trees (one of the largest rookeries on Vancouver Island is in Beacon Hill Park in Victoria)

LOON

- Pacific loon smaller than the common loon and found on the open ocean
- Common loon found on lakes and rivers
- Adults often carry young on their backs for protection

MARBLED MURRELET

- A diving seabird and a threatened species
- Breed inland in coastal old-growth forests—make nests high up in the canopy
- First nest found in Canada was in a Sitka spruce in the Walbran Valley in 1990

Fun Fact

Marbled murrelets are usually only seen in the forest at dawn and dusk, and their nests are most often found in trees that are 300 – 800 years old!

STELLER'S JAY

- Bright blue plumage and a dark crest on their head
- Bold nature and scavenging habits
- Distinctive "shack-shack-shack" call

Trees

Fun Fact

Trees are the longest-living organisms on earth.

ARBUTUS

- Usually have a crooked or leaning trunk
- Reddish-brown, thin, smooth bark, peels off naturally to expose younger, greener bark underneath
- Grow in dry, sunny locations, usually close to the ocean

BIGLEAF MAPLE

- Very big leaves, up to 30 cm wide
- Greyish-brown bark, with shallow grooves when older
- Small, greenish-yellow flowers in spring, which hang down in clusters and are sweet and edible
- Often thickly draped with club moss

DOUGLAS FIR

- Very tall—grow up to 85 m
- Trunk often has few branches, except at top
- Grey-brown bark with lots of resin, becoming deeply grooved and ridged with age

GARRY OAK

- Grayish bark with thick scales and grooves
- Garry-oak meadows once covered much of what is now Victoria
- Garry-oak meadows now endangered ecosystems

SITKA SPRUCE

- Commonly grows up to 70 m
- Needles attached in a spiral fashion
- Bark breaks up into scales

WESTERN HEMLOCK

- Mostly down-sweeping branches
- Nearly flat, soft needles in feathery, flat sprays
- Bark is dark-brown to reddish brown, becoming thick and deeply grooved with age

WESTERN REDCEDAR

- Drooping branches, with trunk often wider at the base
- Grey and very stringy bark
- Can be very long-lived, over 1,000 years
- British Columbia's official tree

CONK (BRACKET OR SHELF FUNGI)

- Are related to the mushroom family
- Are the fruiting body of a wood-decaying fungus
- Are an external signal of wood decay inside the trunk

Fun Fact

Conks create new conks by releasing spores that drift through the air until they land on a tree whose bark is injured.

NURSE LOG

- Fallen, dead tree trunks or stumps that have new, mini-gardens growing on top of them—nursing new plants to life
- When the nurse log rots, the roots of the new trees will be above the ground and the new tree will look like it's standing on stilts. The huge roots above ground are called a "colonnade."

Shrubs, Ferns

HIMALAYAN BLACKBERRY

- Introduced species, now blacklisted—invasive disrupter of native ecosystems
- Sprawling canes (brambles) with piercing thorns
- Sweet edible berries ripen in late summer

TRAILING BLACKBERRY

- Native plant
- Distinguished from Himalayan Blackberry by flower shape and leaf shape (see diagram)
- Lacks the white hairs on the underside of the leaf present in the Himalayan

DEVIL'S CLUB

- Huge, maple-like leaves
- Sprays of red berries (inedible)
- Thrives in low light rainforest
- Leaves can cause an itchy rash if touched

FERNS

- Among the oldest living land plants—about 400 million years old!
- 23 species of ferns in B.C.
- Small brown dots on the underside of the leaves are "sori," the plant's reproductive system

KINNIKINNICK

- Evergreen, mat-forming, native groundcover
- Tiny dark-green, spoon-shaped leaves
- Bright red, round berries (edible, but lacking taste)

MAHONIA (OREGON GRAPE)

- Leaves resemble English holly
- Bright-yellow flower clusters February through April
- Edible blue berries in clusters

SALAL

- Most common shrub on coastal Vancouver Island
- Edible reddish-blue to purple berries

SALMONBERRY

- Pink to reddish-purple flowers
- Berries can be mushy, but are pleasant and edible
- Ripen early (May – June)
- Sometimes confused with thimbleberry

SKUNK CABBAGE

- A favourite food of black bears
- Really smells like skunk!
- Grows in swampy, wet areas

THIMBLEBERRY

- Maple-shaped leaves
- Hairy, thornless stems
- White flowers
- Raspberry-like red fruits
- Distinguishable from salmonberry by leaf shape, flower colour, and tighter, smaller clusters in the fruit

Flowers

CAMAS

- Early blooming blue-flowered lily found in Garry-oak meadows
- Used to grow so abundantly that they were sometimes mistaken for water
- BEWARE! While the common and giant camas are edible, meadow-death camas is highly toxic and can cause death. It is difficult to distinguish one from the other. Do not try to harvest camas bulbs.

FAWN LILY (WHITE, PINK)

- Spring-blooming relative of the camas
- Often found near Garry-oak or arbutus groves

SHOOTING STAR

- Bloom in April and May
- Often found in Garry-oak groves

FIRST NATIONS USES OF PLANTS, TREES, AND INTERTIDAL LIFE

Arbutus. Bark was used to make medicinal preparations, and used as a dye by the Straits Salish.

Bigleaf maple. Coastal peoples used the tree to make dishes and paddles—some groups called it the "paddle tree." Bark was used for baskets and rope.

Camas. An important source of starch in the diet of coastal peoples. Families would gather in camps to dig camas bulbs, then would steam up to 50 kg of bulbs at a time to be eaten right away, or sun-dried for later.

Chiton. The collection, preparation, and consumption of chitons was an important aspect of coastal life, and chitons figure prominently in stories and legend. Some prepared chitons in a cedar box full of fresh water, brought to a boil by adding hot rocks, then dipped the chitons in fish or mammal oil just before eating.

Clam. Clams were also very important to coastal First Nations. Because of their abundance, large quantities of butter clams could be harvested, cooked, then dried and stored for winter use.

Devil's club. A very important medicinal plant, especially the roots and bark. It was used to treat arthritis, ulcers, digestive problems, and diabetes, and also used to make dye and paint.

Douglas fir. Used for spear handles, harpoon shafts, fish hooks. The pitch was used for sealing and caulking and as a medicinal salve.

Garry oak. Coastal peoples burned the undergrowth in Garry-oak meadows to cultivate camas bulbs. Garry-oak bark was used in medicinal preparations and to create dyes.

Hemlock. Coastal peoples carved the easily worked wood into spoons and combs, and used hemlock pitch and bark for medicinal purposes.

Kelp. Coastal peoples took refuge in kelp beds if they were caught on the water in storms, throwing kelp over their vessels to steady them. Kayakers and other boaters still do this sometimes.

Mussels. Mussels were collected by coastal peoples and were an important food, sometimes roasted on coals, steamed in a pit, or boiled. Large mussel shells were sharpened and used as knives and for the pointed tips on whaling harpoons.

Sea anemone. The Nuu-chah-nulth harvested sea anemones in the spring and cooked them by steaming.

Sitka spruce. Coastal peoples used the roots of the Sitka spruce to make hats, baskets, ropes, fishing lines, and twine.

Pitch was used as a waterproofing agent for preparing boats, harpoons, and fishing gear. It also had many medicinal uses. Boughs were used by the Ditidaht in winter-dance ceremonies to protect dancers; it was believed the sharp needles gave protection from evil thoughts.

Skunk cabbage. First Nations peoples used leaves as a "wax" paper to line baskets for carrying food.

Sea urchin. Sea urchins were known as "sea eggs," and the edible insides were considered by many as delicacies.

Swordfern. Coastal peoples used swordferns to line boxes and baskets.

Western redcedar. A very important tree for coastal peoples (known as the "tree of life"). All of the tree could be used, and because it was easy to split and rot-resistant, it was favoured for cultural items, including canoes, house planks, boxes, clothing, masks, paddles, rope, cradles, and baskets.

Whale. The traditional whaling season for coastal peoples was in May and June. The whale was extremely important both for its many practical uses (oil, meat, sinew, and bone), and for its ceremonial significance.

MAPS, BOOKS, AND WEBSITES

Topographical Maps

Crown Publications, Victoria, B.C. Tel: 250-386-4636 (to check availability of topographical maps).

Books

CAMPING WITH CHILDREN

Boga, Steve. *Camping and Backpacking with Children.* Mecanicsburg, PA: Stackpole Books, 1995.

Cary, Alice. *Parents' Guide to Hiking and Camping: A Trailside Guide.* New York, NY: W.W. Norton & Company, 1997.

Foster, Lynne. *Take a Hike! The Sierra Club Kids Guide to Hiking and Backpacking.* San Francisco, CA: Sierra Club Books, 1991.

Hodgson, Michael. *Wilderness with Children: A Parent's Guide to Fun Family Outings.* Harrisburg, PA: Stackpole Books, 1992.

Kraiker, Rolf and Debra. *Cradle to Canoe: Camping and Canoeing with Children.* Erin, ON: The Boston Mills Press, 1999.

McLean, Celia. *Hiking the Rockies With Kids.* Victoria, BC: Orca Books, 1992.

Ross, Cindy and Todd Gladfelter. *Kids in the Wild: A Family Guide to Outdoor Recreation.* Seattle, WA: Mountaineers Books, 1995.

Tawney, Robin. *Hiking With Kids: Taking Those First Steps With Young Hikers.* Helena, MO: Falcon Publishing, 2000.

Woodson, Roger and Kimberley. *The Parent's Guide to Camping With Children.* Cincinnatti, OH: Betterway Books, 1995.

NATURE APPRECIATION WITH CHILDREN

Carson, Rachel. *The Sense of Wonder.* New York, NY: HarperCollins, 1998.

Cornell, Joseph. *Sharing Nature With Children.* Nevada City, CA: New Dawn Publications, 1979.

Doherty, Paul. *Backyard Stars: A Guide For Home and The Road.* Palo Alto, CA: A Klutz Guide, 1998.

Nabhan, Gary and Stephen Trimble. *The Geography of Childhood: Why Children Need Wild Places.* Boston, MA: Beacon Press, 1994.

CHILDREN'S ACTIVITIES

Sher, Barbara. *Self-Esteem Games: 300 Activities That Make Children Feel Good About Themselves.* New York, NY: John Wiley & Sons Ltd., 1998.

BACKPACKING

Curtis, Rick. *The Backpacker's Field Manual: A Comprehensive Guide to Mastering Backcountry Skills.* New York, NY: Three Rivers Press, 1998.

Kelty, Nena and Steve Boga. *Backpacking the Kelty Way.* New York, NY: Perigee Books, 2000.

Ross, Cindy and Todd Gladfelter. *A Hiker's Companion: 12,000 Miles of Trail-tested Wisdom.* Seattle, WA: The Mountaineers, 1993.

Townsend, Chris. *The Backpacker's Handbook* (2nd edition). Camden, ME: Ragged Mountain Press, 1997.

OLYMPIC NATIONAL PARK

Hooper, David. *Exploring Washington's Wild Olympic Coast*. Seattle, WA: The Mountaineers, 1993.

McNulty, Tim. *Olympic National Park: A Natural History Guide*. New York, NY: Houghton Mifflin, 1996.

Molvar, Erik. *Hiking Olympic National Park*. Helena, MO: Falcon Publishing, 1995.

Wood, Robert L. *Olympic Mountains Trail Guide: National Park and National Forest*. Seattle, WA: The Mountaineers, 2000.

———. *The Land That Slept Late: The Olympic Mountains in Legend and History*. Seattle, WA: The Mountaineers, 1995.

Gilmore, Robert. *Great Walks: The Olympic Peninsula*. Goffstown, NH: Great Walks, Inc., 1999.

VANCOUVER ISLAND

Blier, Richard. *Hiking Trails II: Victoria and Vicinity*. Victoria, BC: Vancouver Island Trails Information Society, 1993.

Cowan, Shannon and Lissa. *Hiking Vancouver Island: A Guide To Vancouver Island's Greatest Hiking Adventures*. Guildford, CT: Globe Pequot Press, 2003.

Gill, Ian. *Hiking on the Edge: West Coast Trail, Juan de Fuca Trail*. Vancouver, BC: Raincoast Books, 1995.

Lansdowne, Helen. *Nature Walks Around Victoria*. Vancouver, BC: Greystone Books, 1999.

Lawrence, Susan, ed. *Hiking Trails 1: Victoria and Vicinity*. Victoria, BC: Vancouver Island Trails Information Society, 1997.

Leadem, Tim. *The West Coast Trail and Other Great Hikes*. Vancouver, BC: Greystone Books, 1998.

MacFarlane, J.M. et al. *Official Guide to Pacific Rim National Park Reserve*. Calgary, AB: Blackbird Naturgraphics, 1996.

Mills, Donald. *Giant Cedars White Sands: Juan de Fuca Marine Trail Guidebook*. Sooke, BC: D. Mills Publisher, 1999.

Vasilevich, Adam and Matthew Payne. *The Juan de Fuca Marine Trail: A Hikers Guide to the Land and Its Inhabitants*. Vancouver, BC: Unnum Press, 1997.

PLANTS AND ANIMALS OF THE PACIFIC NORTHWEST

Archer, Karen. *Beach Creatures: Intertidal Plants and Animals to Find and Draw*. Saltspring Island, BC: M. Hepburn & Associates Inc., 1994.

Burt, William Henry. *Peterson Field Guide to the Mammals*. Boston, MA: Houghton Mifflin Company, 1980.

Harbo, Rick M. *Whelks to Whales: Coastal Marine Life of the Pacific Northwest*. Vancouver, BC: Harbour Publishing, 1999.

———. *Tidepool and Reef Marine Guide to the Pacific Northwest Coast*. Surrey, BC: Hancock House Publishers Ltd., 1980.

Fisher, Chris C. *West Coast Birds*. Vancouver. BC: Lone Pine Publishing, 1996.

East of Sombrio Beach on the Juan de Fuca Trail

Peterson, Roger Tory. *A Field Guide to Western Birds*. New York, NY: Houghton Mifflin Company, 1990.

Sept, J. Duane. *The Beachcombers Guide to Seashore Life in the Pacific Northwest*. Vancouver, BC: Harbour Publishing, 1999.

Cannings, Richard and Sidney Cannings. *British Columbia: A Natural History*. Vancouver, BC: Greystone Books, 1996.

Sheldon, Ian. *Seashore of British Columbia*. Vancouver, BC: Lone Pine Publishing, 1998.

FIRST NATIONS LORE AND HISTORY

Challenger, Robert James. *Orca's Family and More Northwest Coast Stories*. Surrey, BC: Heritage House Publishing Company, 1997.

Coull, Cheryl. *A Traveller's Guide To Aboriginal B.C.* Vancouver, BC: Whitecap Books, 1996.

Elliott, Dave. *Saltwater People*. Victoria, BC: School District 63 (Saanich), 1990.

Ellis, David and Luke Swan. *Teachings of the Tides: Uses of Marine Invertebrates By The Manhousat People*. Nanaimo, BC: Theytus Books, 1981.

Woodcock, George. *The Peoples of the Coast: The Indians of the Pacific Northwest*. Bloomington, IN: Indiana University Press, 1977.

COOKING

Axcell, Claudia et al. *Simple Foods for The Pack*. San Francisco, CA: Sierra Club Books, 1986.

Daniel, Linda. *Kayak Cookery: A Handbook of Provisions and Recipes*. Chester, CT: The Globe Pequot Press, 1986.

Kozloff, Eugene N. *Plants and Animals of the Pacific Northwest: An Illustrated Guide to the Natural History of Western Oregon, Washington, and British Columbia*. Vancouver, BC: Greystone Books, 1995.

MacKinnon, Andy and Jim Pojar. *Plants of Coastal British Columbia including Washington, Oregon and Alaska*. Vancouver, BC: Lone Pine Publishing, 1994.

Parish, Roberts and Sandra Thomson. *Tree Book: Learning to Recognize Trees of British Columbia*. Victoria, BC: Canadian Forest Service, Ministry of Forests.

McHugh, Gretchen. *The Hungry Hiker's Book of Good Cooking*. Toronto, ON: Knopf, 1982.

Miller, Dorcas S. *Backcountry Cooking: From Pack to Plate in 10 Minutes*. Seattle, WA: The Mountaineers, 1998.

——. *Good Food For Camp and Trail: All-Natural Recipes For Delicious Meals Outdoors*. Boulder, CO: Pruett Publishing Co., 1993.

Pearson, Claudia. *National Outdoor Leadership School Cookery*. Mecanicsburg, PA: Stackpole Books, 1997.

Yaffe, Linda. *High Trail Cookery: All-Natural, Home-Dried, Palate-Pleasing Meals for the Backpacker*. Chicago, IL: Chicago Review Press, 1989.

Websites

B.C. PROVINCIAL PARKS
Official BC Parks site. Downloadable park brochures, all fee information.

http://wlapwww.gov.bc.ca/bcparks/explore/explore.htm

CAPITAL REGIONAL DISTRICT PARKS
Trail descriptions, ratings, driving instructions, downloadable maps, photos for each park, and even a link to the federal government tide tables.

http://www.crd.bc.ca/parks/

CLUBTREAD
ClubTread is an online community dedicated to the outdoors and focussed mainly on B.C. hiking. On their site, you will find a searchable park/trail database, trip reports, discussion forums, and gear for sale. A great way to get first-hand info on trails, as well as access to excellent photos. Beware! You could waste a lot of time on this site dreaming about future hikes …

http://www.clubtread.com/

LEAVE NO TRACE
Leave No Trace is a non-profit organization that promotes and inspires responsible outdoor recreation through education, research and partnerships. The Leave No Trace program builds awareness, appreciation, and respect for our wild lands and is dedicated to creating a nationally recognized and accepted outdoor ethic that incorporates both personal responsibility and land stewardship.

http://www.lnt.org/

OLYMPIC NATIONAL PARK
Officially the site for a shuttle service in the park, this site has everything—over 1,500 photos, trail descriptions, personal trip reports, links to tide tables, accommodation info, and more.

www.windsox.us/menu.html

U.S. NATIONAL PARKS
The official U.S. National Parks site also has excellent trail information for Olympic National Park, and up-to-date info on all fees, regulations, and services. Click on "In-Depth" to access the backcountry section of the site, which includes photos and some great educational resources (Note: navigating this site can be confusing.)

http://www.nps.gov/olym/

About the authors

Kari Jones and Sachiko Kiyooka are writers and mothers who are passionate about the outdoors and sharing the gifts of nature with their little ones. They have gone wilderness camping all over the world, but have a special love for the beauty of the west coast and all its treasures.